"You intended to
accomplish what is ┊

Genesis 50:20

INTENDED
HARM

*Intended Harm was previously published under the pseudonym, Jurney
Eve. This new edition includes excerpts from her kidnapper's ex-wife.

INTENDED HARM

My Escape, Denial, Healing and Forgiveness

DIANA OAKLEY

Another Quality Book Published By:

LEGACY BOOK PUBLISHING

1883 Lee Road, Winter Park, FL 32789

www.LEGACYBOOKPUBLISHING.com

Intended Harm: My Escape, Denial, Healing and Forgiveness

Published by:
LEGACY Book Publishing
1883 Lee Road
Winter Park, Florida 32789
www.LegacyBookPublishing.com

© Diana Oakley 2012
Printed in the United States
ISBN: 978-1-937952-12-9

Cover Design by Gabriel H. Vaughn

I dedicate this book
to all those who have been kidnapped,
and never had a chance
to tell their story.

The Oak

In a meadow far away, I sat upon a hill,
The sun was warm, the breeze was light, the birds were calm and still.
I sat beneath a single oak, with limbs that reached out long,
The breeze blew through the dangling leaves and sang to me a song.

"For I, the tree, can tell, that you are feeling blue,
No matter what it is, I know I can help you...
I'm old and wise and rooted here, upon this earth by God,
For souls like yours to get away, and sit upon my sod.
So tell me, lone and lovely one, what's it that bothers you?
I sense you question love and trust, in a world filled with confuse."

"I feel alone", I answered back, "I feel that no one cares,
Not just for me, but in this world, that seems so full of terrors...
What's the point of being here, if only just to leave?
Any why we're made to feel these blues, I just cannot conceive."

"God put you here for reasons, dear, for this, there is no doubt,
And when it's time for you to go, the Lord will take you out.
Alone, should you never feel, for someone's always there,
You must believe the words of God, and that He always cares.
You have a special Angel, that guards you every day,
And when you wish to speak to me, my leaves shall always sway."

I awoke to the sound of a bird in chirp, and within the oak, I lay,
Right upon a swinging branch, back and forth it sway.
It rocked me for a minute more, and stopped as I sat up,
It lowered down to the ground, and opened up its cup.
The leaves were rustling quietly, although no breeze was there,
I said my thanks, and then I left, with feeling no despair.
Now, when I'm blue, I close my eyes, and to the oak I go,
With a gentle breeze and swaying leaves, and a bough to hold me close.

~Stacie Lewis
2000

Table of Contents

"You intended to harm me, but God intended it for good to accomplish what is now being done, the saving of many lives."

Genesis 50:20

Introduction

You are about to read my personal blog. It is my story about how I was abducted and raped by a stranger when I was seventeen years old. Writing it was one of the hardest things I have ever done. It is written from my perspective and my blog entries do not reflect the views of others. Some of the details might not be entirely accurate but I *will* tell you that, to the best of my knowledge and memory, the events as I tell them in my story, are true. I have changed the names of the people in my story for their protection. You will understand why as you read.

When this first happened to me in 1991, all I wanted to do was pretend it didn't happen. Of course, I couldn't pretend with myself but to everybody else I acted like it didn't happen. Inside I was angry at everybody. I was angry at my friends for not being more comforting and supportive but at the same time I was angry with them when they tried to talk about it. I was screaming inside because I wanted to talk about it but I didn't want to bring my pain to the surface. I wasn't ready to deal with it.

Sixteen years passed by before I finally opened up and started talking about what had happened and I can honestly say that I wish I had done it sooner. I know it sounds cliché but I feel so much better now. When I told my story, people opened up to me and told me their story. It helped to hear their pain. It helped to know that someone else knew what I was going through. It helped to know that I wasn't alone. Now all I want to do is help others.

By reading my story, you will find out that what this man did to me not only impacted *my* life, but the life of his wife and child. I was fortunate enough to have his now ex-wife, Renee share some of her memories with us as well.

If you take only one thing away from my story I hope it is this…this man used me. He hurt me to satisfy his own desires, but God has shown me how to rise above my pain and use it to help others. God has taught me a lot about myself and about love, life and forgiveness. Yes, I have forgiven the man who abducted me, raped me and intended to kill me. That might be difficult for some of you to understand but I hope after you read my story you will.

I would also like to clarify that I am not telling this because I want you to feel sorry for me. I am sharing my story to let you know that this did not destroy me. For sixteen years I thought that this did destroy me. I thought I would never be a "normal" person with "normal" relationships and "normal" fears and "normal" expectations. But you know what? What is "normal"? We all have our own unique stories to tell. Stories about how we've overcome adversity. How we've been faced with tough decisions. Without our trials we would never learn. We would never grow. I hope that if you read my story, you'll look at your own life with a new attitude and understanding as to why bad things have happened to you. Maybe it will help you overcome *your* past.

I truly believe that God never gives us more than we can handle. It's how we handle what He gives us that make us who we are.

"When you make a vow to God, do not delay in fulfilling it. He has no pleasure in fools; fulfill your vow."

Ecclesiastes 5:4

Lately, I've had an overwhelming feeling to write about a very personal thing that happened to me. I don't know why but I feel like I'm *supposed* to tell people this story. It's a very hard story for me to tell for many reasons. First, this is something I have tried to forget about for a really long time. It took me sixteen years to realize that forgetting about it wouldn't make me whole again. Remembering has actually made me stronger.

Second, I don't like "letting people in." What happened to me was very publicized and humiliating. By writing about it, it would be publicized again but NOT humiliating. It took me many years to realize that I had no reason to be ashamed. It wasn't my fault. The only person who is to blame is the man who kidnapped me.

The funny thing is, the more I think about what I'm going to write, and how I'm going to write it, the less real it becomes to me and the easier it becomes. It almost feels like it didn't happen to me at all. It becomes this fictitious story from an anonymous author.

Another reason I am hesitant to tell my story is because the person that did this to me is sitting in prison, probably envisioning ways to find me once he is released. I guess he holds me accountable instead of himself.

"The Lord is close to the brokenhearted and saves those who are crushed in spirit."

Psalm 34:18

Religion

I've decided I had better give you a little more background before I tell you my story. I think that for you to truly appreciate this story you must know a little about my religious teachings as a child.

I didn't come from a religious family. I can't remember ever seeing a family member go to church, other than my brothers and me. Nobody in my family ever told me about God or any of the Bible stories. The only time I ever heard about God was in the occasional Sunday school class. Once Sunday was over I didn't hear about Him until the next Sunday.

When I became a teenager, I started going to a youth group on Wednesday evenings but it was not to learn about God. It was because that was the only way I would get to see my boyfriend. He went to a different school district and we lived about 10 miles away from each other. A girls gotta do what a girls gotta do, right?

Now, what you have to understand is that just because I went to church occasionally did not mean I was a good kid. I was a rotten kid! I went to youth group to make out with my boyfriend in the back of the church van. I'm surprised they let me go at all. It's not like we were discreet. But I know that something good did come out of my church excursions. When I was in third grade, I prayed that prayer to ask Jesus to come into my heart and I became a born-again Christian. I really meant it at the time but once I left the church that day everything went back to "normal". It wasn't until 1999 that I recommitted my life to Christ.

In between 1982 and 1999 I was very, very far from what you would call a Christian, but I always felt God with me very faintly. It's hard to explain. Every so often I would feel God's pull even when I was in my darkest hours...especially, when I was in my darkest hours. I'm telling you this because I want you to know that I believe that God had a plan for me. I gave my heart to Him in third grade and He never forgot about me. It taught me that you can turn your back on God but God will never turn His back on you.

"But we also rejoice in our sufferings, because we know that suffering produces perseverance; perseverance, character; and character, hope."

Romans 5:3

Event Horizon

Isn't it strange how one event can define who you are for the rest of your life? Well, maybe not define who you are but definitely alter you in significant ways. It can alter the way you do things. It can alter your actions, your thoughts, your relationships. What happened to me has altered me in many ways.

I do things that I don't think "normal" people do. Here are a few examples? I climb all the way into the car to buckle my daughter into her car seat because I'm afraid someone will come up to me from behind and attack me. I also don't like sitting with my back to anyone and I won't if I can help it. I can't drive my car without the doors locked. I lock them immediately upon entering. I'm almost obsessive about making sure all my windows and doors are locked in my house. If I know that my front door was unlocked and unsupervised, I will check every nook and cranny of my house. If I go to someone's house who doesn't ever lock their doors, (Oh yeah, they're out there) I have a hard time relaxing. I can't leave windows open. I have a really hard time letting my children spend the night at other people's houses.

Unfortunately, I could go on and on, but I won't. I just wanted to try to explain to you how this event has completely altered my life. I'm sure all of us have had a significant event happen to them that's shaped them into the person they are today. Mine happened on April 28th, 1991.

"Peace I leave with you; my peace I give you. I do not give to you as the world gives. Do not let your hearts be troubled and do not be afraid."

John 14:27

-My Kidnapper's Wife

Jim and I were married in 1987 on Valentine's Day and we welcomed our beautiful baby girl, Tara two years later. The day I found out I was pregnant, I rushed out to Wagner's bakery to buy a cake with one pink and one blue bootie and the words "Congratulations Daddy!" on it. I was never happier. Life would be wonderful from that day on.

Our little bundle of joy arrived the first week in August, 1989. Epidurals were brand new on the scene in that year and I wasn't taking any risks with "new procedures", so I opted for a natural, drug free delivery. Well, forty hours later Miss Tara made her appearance.

Jim was there through it all, always positive, always encouraging. When Tara arrived he stayed right by her side. He even gave her her first bath.

He would sit and rock her for hours. He was so happy. I can even remember the smile on his face.

We moved out of the one bedroom apartment, and bought an eighty foot long, fourteen foot wide mobile home. We moved out to the country. We had our own space, two cars, two jobs, a beautiful home, and great new friends. Life couldn't have been better. Jim took Tara with him everywhere he went. They were inseparable. He always had her by his side, they even went fishing together. The one thing I will always be able to say is that he was a very good daddy to our little girl.

I'm not sure when things started to go wrong. I guess it's harder to see it happening when it's happening to you. Jim would always sing my praises to others but, in private, he became very critical of me. He was always correcting me. Just a little bit at first, but growing little by little over time, spreading like a cancer. I began to feel inferior, incompetent. I started questioning my intelligence. How is it that I could excel at work but be such an utter failure at home? Always correcting, always chastising, always belittling. It wears you down and makes you believe you are as worthless as they say you are.

I often thought about divorce, but the relationship wasn't physically abusive. I guess I had convinced myself that as long as he wasn't physically abusive, then it was okay. I was raised in the church. I was a born again Christian. I believed that the man ran the household. Divorce wasn't an acceptable option in my mind. But I grew unhappier by the day.

I remember one day Jim came home from work. I had been home all day. I had cleaned the house from one end to the other. Now, with a baby in the house you know what a feat this could be. I was proud of myself, and of the way the house looked. Jim came home and found flour finger prints on the handle of the microwave and went ballistic. He put his hands around my neck and started to shake me back and forth. He started yelling at me and telling me how useless I was. Asking me why I couldn't even manage to clean correctly. My sister Kerrie just happened to walk up my driveway at that moment. She never realized what she interrupted that day, but I was certainly thankful for her arrival.

That was the day I began to grow a backbone. I started paying attention. I started questioning. That was the day I stopped taking my husband's word at face value. I loved this man but something wasn't right. I began watching carefully for any signs with Tara. If he was capable of abusing me emotionally as well as physically, what could be going on with the baby? I couldn't even entertain the thought that he would hurt the baby. He loved her, doted on her. He was so proud of her. But that's how he was with me at first too.

I worked for a company that was in the process of closing down all of their stores in the US. I had been promoted to a regional manager and had been working on new store setups and openings that kept me traveling. But after I had had the baby and the company announced that it was pulling out of the American marketplace, my choices were limited. I could go on the road and help close down the stores, or I could go on unemployment. We chose to go on the road.

So, we packed up the baby and moved to New Jersey. Jim and Tara would spend the days on the beach while I was at work, and we would have as normal a life as we could when I wasn't working. When I finally worked myself out of a job in January, we returned home, and Jim had to go to work. As I write this, I wonder how many unsolved rapes are on the books in New Jersey from the fall of 1990 till January 1991.

Jim worked as a "roofer". He would often take me to houses and say "See what I did!" He was always very proud of his work. I would smile and say how nice it was but I was completely dumb founded by it all. I hadn't seen what it looked like before he started it. I didn't see it in progress, and honestly, it looked like a roof. Like every other one on the street.

As I began to question things in my mind, lots of thing didn't add up. Jim would show up at home with items he would take in trade for roofing work he would do. Items such as camcorders, cameras, a generator, and all these odd items would begin to make their way into our spare room. He never had a use for any of them; they would just sit and take up space. He never had a use for any of the items he brought home. It was just stuff. I would ask why he traded for a generator, but it made him angry. "What does it matter? I got paid", was his answer. I had a friend who used to work in law enforcement. I asked him to look into whether or not any of these things had been reported stolen. Something just wasn't sitting right with me.

My dad had told us that if we wanted to clear a patch of his land, we could build a house there. So, every chance we got Jim insisted that we go up to Davis Road and work at clearing the land. We spent a lot of time out there in the woods. We would take the gun and do some target shooting. We would clear the trees and brush, and burn it. Often the flames would get so tall I was in fear that we would set the entire woods on fire. I didn't dare give voice to my fears for fear of his response. I became so afraid of Jim that I tucked a note in the depths of my wallet that I always carried in my back pocket that read "If I am found dead, my husband Jim killed me"

Jim began going to town late at night, quite often taking Tara with him and leaving me at home wondering where he was and whether or not he would be coming back with her. I began spending hours agonizing over leaving him. I began praying. I prayed that God would remove him from me. I asked him to take him away, put him somewhere else. I just needed peace.

"Do not despise the Lord's discipline and do not resent rebuke, because the Lord disciplines those he loves."

Proverbs 3: 11 & 12

Idle Hands

April 28, 1991 was a Sunday morning, but this was no ordinary Sunday morning. This was the day that would change my life. It was also the morning after I'd finally worked up the courage to tell Mark that I liked him. I told him at a party on a balcony surrounded by kids from our school and strangers from a few neighboring schools. I don't know what I was thinking. How embarrassing would it have been if he had rejected me? He didn't reject me, but he didn't entirely swoon either. I couldn't tell if he liked me or if he just didn't want to hurt my feelings in front of everyone. Either way, we exchanged phone numbers before he had to leave. He was sixteen and he had a curfew. Me, on the other hand, well I'm sure I had a curfew...in my mother's eyes...but I pretty much came and went as I pleased.

I was seventeen, rebellious, disrespectful. The kind of kid that every parent of a rebellious teenager hopes they have when they have kids of their own. You know the type. I am pretty sure my mom wasn't telling stories about how wonderful I was to her co-workers or anything. On a side note...Mom, I'm sorry. If it's any consolation I think I will get a taste of that teenage rebellion from at least one of my kids.

So, here it is, Sunday morning and I really wanted to call Mark but I figured it was too soon for that. I wanted to talk to him, maybe even see him but I didn't know how that would be possible without looking too desperate. We didn't have any mutual friends so I couldn't stage a chance encounter or anything like that. I had all but given up on any chance of seeing him again until Monday morning at school, when I decided to take a bike ride.

I rode my bike a lot. I loved riding my bike. I loved to take long bike rides all by myself on rarely traveled country roads with nothing but the sounds of nature around me. I couldn't have made a much easier target. What an idiot! Anyway...there was something so peaceful about being by myself. It was silent and I always appreciated silence.

Mark lived seven miles away in a little town with a park that I knew he went to often with his friends to play basketball. It was a fourteen mile round trip which was no problem for me. I figured, I'd ride to the park and back. Maybe I'd get lucky. What else did I have to do?

"In God I trust; I will not be afraid. What can man do to me?"

Psalms 56:11

Intuition

It was the first nice weekend we'd had since spring started and it was the perfect day for a bike ride. I wore a pair of cut-off jean shorts, a tank top and a flannel. Don't laugh! It was the 90's, remember? Flannels were cool.

The ride to the park was uneventful. I don't know how long it took me to travel the first seven miles. I didn't pay attention to the time. When I finally got to the park, Mark wasn't there. I waited about thirty minutes, hoping he would show, but eventually I gave up and headed for home.

The road that connected our two towns had a few hills on it, and I admit, I walked my bike up one or two of them. There were about three dozen houses on this seven mile stretch of road, but one house in particular drew my attention more than the others. The house was on one of those hills I previously mentioned, and I was walking my bike. There were a few men working on the roof and they stopped to look at me. Now, I've been stared at by men before in my life, what female hasn't, but this was different. Something seemed wrong. I felt very uncomfortable, so I walked faster. Once I was far enough away from the house, the uncomfortable feeling went away. I brushed it off, thinking I had overreacted. I can be kind of a drama queen.

I never gave that moment much thought after that until fifteen years later when I found out that my attacker was a "roofer". Maybe he was one of those men working on the roof. Maybe that's where he first saw me. Maybe we looked at each other as I walked by. Looking back on that moment, I can't believe I ignored the feeling of foreboding that I experienced there. It was an overwhelming feeling to run and hide. Maybe it was God trying to warn me. But where would I have gone? I was five miles from home and it was before the cell phone era. Maybe God was trying to prepare me for the inevitable. I have let that thought dance through my head once or twice over the years. They say things happen for a reason, right? I still haven't figured out what that reason could be but the older I get, the more open I am to this theory. Maybe it's not the older I get. Maybe it's just the more time that passes.

Well, if God *was* trying to prepare me, it was in vain because nothing could have prepared me for what happened next.

"For God did not give us a spirit of timidity, but a spirit of power, of love and of self-discipline."

2 Timothy 1: 7

Ignorance

At the top of the hill I got back on my bike and continued riding. There was a two mile hill coming up and I was looking forward to coasting down it. Despite the fact that I didn't get to see Mark, I was having a great day. I was coasting down the hill and going pretty fast when all of a sudden, something very hard hit the back of my head and sent me flying off my bike. I skidded about thirty feet across the pavement.

When I looked up, I saw a red pickup truck parked on the side of the road. A man got out of the driver's seat and ran over to me. He was an older, unattractive man with a weak chin and a large gut that hung over his pants. He asked me if I was alright. He seemed concerned and upset that he had hit me. I called him an asshole. I remember being a little shocked that I had just called him an asshole, but at the time it seemed appropriate. I mean, he just hit me with his truck. If there were ever a time to call someone an asshole it was then.

He was very apologetic, which made me feel guilty about my outburst. I truly believed it was an accident and that he was sorry. He offered to take me to the hospital. I was trying to think clearly but it was difficult. I felt my head and it was bleeding. Should I let him take me to the hospital or should I go to the closest house and call 911? There were two houses that were about fifty yards from where we were and I knew that two girls from my school lived in them. I'm sure I could have used one of their phones.

He asked me where I lived. I told him I lived about two miles from where we were. He said he'd take me to my house if I wanted. The thought of being safe with my mom was comforting. She could take me to the hospital.

He took advantage of my temporary confusion and before I could say yes to his last offer, he put my bike into the back of his truck. He gently, but quickly helped me up and walked me over to his truck. I got into the passenger's seat. It was the passenger's side mirror that hit me on the back of my head and knocked me off my bike.

I was bleeding pretty badly and I could feel a small crack when I touched the back of my head. He gave me a t-shirt to put against my head and he asked me where I lived...and I told him. He was trying to comfort me. He told me we'd call an ambulance from my house. He said everything was going to be alright. He was so sorry. Blah, blah, blah!

About a mile from my house he "suddenly" realized that he didn't have his driver's license or his registration with him. He asked me if it would be alright if we went to his house first so he could get them. He said it was about one mile up the street. He said he'd get into so much more trouble if he didn't have them with him when the police were called. He told me his wife was home and that she was a nurse. She could take a quick look at my head. Now, I didn't have my license yet. I had no idea that this was not such a big problem. I mean, this man who seemed so concerned about me. Who seemed so troubled by what he had done; so comforting; so helpful. I, surprisingly, wasn't in too much pain at that moment. Maybe I wasn't hurt as bad as I thought I was. I could let him stop at his house real quick to pick up his license and registration. I didn't want to. I wanted to get to my mom as soon as possible but he seemed so worried about it that I said it would be alright.

I felt safe at that moment with my comforter...my abductor.

"But you be strong and do not lose courage, for there is reward for your work."

2 Chronicles 15:7

All In

We drove right through the center of town. There must have been something big going on because there were a lot of people all walking in the same direction. I saw my best friend, Danyelle's, mom in the crowd and I almost started crying harder. I just really wanted to be there with her on that sidewalk. It was as if my subconscious sensed something was wrong even though my conscious self didn't and I wanted to get out of the truck.

To this day, even though I haven't seen Danyelle's mom in years and years, I still feel a strong bond to her. Maybe it's because she was always so kind and welcoming toward me. Maybe it's because she was the last friendly face I saw. Whatever it was, that was when I started to feel uneasy. I assured myself that I was over-reacting. What could possibly go wrong? This man was helping me. He had a picture of his wife and kid attached to the passenger side visor. He was a dad. When I asked him a question about his daughter he smiled and told me that she was two years old. She liked Elmo and he beamed with pride. This man wasn't going to hurt me. I was definitely over-reacting

By the time we turned down "his road" my feelings were changing toward my new "friend". Although he tried to keep the conversation light with casual questions like, "What grade are you in?" I'd say, "Tenth". "Do you like school?" "Sure." He even asked me if I would babysit his daughter sometime. But something wasn't right. He told me his house was just up the road but we had driven at least another five miles and made a few turns. Now we were in the middle of nowhere. There were no houses.

I felt like I was "all in" at the poker table. You know what I mean? When all your chips are in the pile and it's too late to take them out and there's nothing you can do but hope and pray for the best. I was in the middle of nowhere with a t-shirt pressed firmly against my cracked skull. I was "all in."

"Cast all your anxiety on Him for He cares for you."

1 Peter 5: 7

The Ruse

He made a right turn into what appeared to be an empty field. There was a slightly worn path leading into it to indicate that a vehicle had previously driven there which made his next statement seem somewhat credible in my naive mind. As if sensing my anxiety, he said, "Don't worry. This is my driveway. We just had the house built so the driveway's not done yet."

As I write this, I am amazed at how naive I was. I WAS only seventeen. I lived in a very small town where nothing bad ever seemed to happen and I also was bleeding from a crack in my skull. I like to pretend that my lack of judgment was affected by my loss of blood. That makes me feel a little better. Of course, at this point, what was there to do but hope he was telling the truth? It wouldn't have mattered if he had turned on me right at that moment. I was cornered.

We drove past a piece of rusting farm equipment and he said something like, "Why did my brother leave this here?" As if farm equipment was more important than this girl he'd almost killed with his truck! He actually stopped the truck and got out to examine it. I remember thinking, "Farmers...humph?!?"

He opened the back of his truck, got something out, closed it back up, came over to my door, opened it and said something. I don't remember clearly what he said because I was too busy looking at the hatchet in his hand. I think he said, "Don't scream!" or something to that affect. What I do remember, very vividly, is the feeling of complete helplessness and disbelief. It washed over me, as if he was pouring it on my head. I could feel it cascading down my entire body.

Fight or flight? I couldn't do either. I was cornered. He was probably marveling at his luck. He couldn't have chosen a more gullible target. What an idiot I was! How could I have let this happen?!?

"My eyes have grown dim with grief; my whole frame is but a shadow."

Job 17: 7

Introverted

He made me get out of the truck so he could tie my hands behind my back with some rope that he later claimed to just have lying around his truck. He had me sit back down in the passenger's seat and he told me to put my head between my knees. It was apparent to me that he was going to drive somewhere else and he didn't want me to see where.

He got back into the driver's seat and he said, "See this? This is an ice pick. Do you know what would happen if I stabbed you in the chest with this? It would puncture your lung and it'd fill up with blood and you'd drown in your own blood."

Wow! That was more information than was necessary. He had me at "Don't scream!"

So I did what I was told and I put my head between my knees. We drove around for what felt like twenty minutes while I stared at the floor and the ice pick's sharp point pressed against my ribcage. I remember seeing a half a dozen shotgun shells rolling around on the floor at my feet and I thought...he must be a hunter. In fact, the strangest thoughts were going through my mind during those twenty minutes. Thoughts you would not think would occur to someone who was in my situation but they were there regardless.

I thought of Danyelle's mom. I wondered what she was doing. I wondered what she was going to make for dinner that night. I ate at Danyelle's house frequently, so I guess I was wondering what I would be missing out on. I wondered if my mom was worried about me yet. She probably wasn't. She was used to me leaving and not coming home until much later, if I even came home at all. This made me feel worse. No one was going to notice my absence! I remember thinking; Mark is never going to go out with me after this! If I survive this, that is. I was trying to think of anything other than my current situation.

He was talking to me. I was aware of his voice but I was only listening to myself. I was, once again, running away from my problem, except this time, instead of physically running away I was psychologically running away.

"Jesus wept."

John 11:35

Desecration

When the truck finally stopped and he told me I could sit up, I saw that we were in the woods. I looked around in every direction and all I could see were trees...lots of trees. I couldn't quite tell which direction we'd driven in from because there were tire tracks coming from both directions and he had pulled his truck off of the path so that it was perpendicular to it. Since I wasn't paying attention to anything other than my own comforting thoughts, I didn't take notice to the motions of the truck as we were driving there.

At that point, I had completely surrendered. I knew he had brought me there to rape me. I'm not sure how I knew that. Had he told me that or had I just assumed? I could only hope that he would not kill me as well. I knew my chances of that were pretty small. I had seen his face. I was seventeen. I wasn't a small child who might not be able to identify him later. But I didn't give up the hope that I might live through this.

I won't go into too much detail as to what happened in the next two hours but I will say...he raped me...many times.

There was a small clearing in the woods in front of the truck and he laid down a blanket that he just happened to have lying around his truck. I tried to disassociate my mind from my body. I kept telling myself that he wasn't raping me. He was raping someone else. I was like an actress in a movie. He directed me and I performed for him.

Man, that sounds so wrong!

Over the course of my captivity, he told me he was thinking about taking me to his brother. His brother would LOVE this, he said. How disgusting! Knowing that there were two of them out there was terribly unsettling. Obviously, his brother was just as sick as he was. I could see his mind working, wondering if it would be possible to take me to his brother, but in the end, he'd decided against it.

He also revealed to me that this was much better than the last time when he'd raped the little girl. This was even more disgusting than what he was doing to me. He had done this to a child?!? He told me she was ten years old. I asked him if he had let her live and he didn't answer me. Why wouldn't he answer me? I started analyzing his silence. If I knew that he didn't kill her, maybe I wouldn't be so afraid of him. But if he did kill her, maybe I would fight him.

That was the only time he mentioned the little girl but I couldn't stop thinking about her. I convinced myself that his silence meant that he had killed her and my heart mourned for her.

"Trust in the Lord with all your heart, and lean not on your own understanding; in all your ways acknowledge Him, and He will make your paths straight."

Proverbs 3: 5 - 6

My Escape

When what felt like an eternity had passed, he stood back and stared at me for a while...as if contemplating what to do next. After a few minutes, he took my shorts and put them on over my head so that they were covering my face. He told me not to take them off and under no circumstance was I to look over at the truck. This demand was unusual. The only other time he had "blinded" me was that time in the field and that was because he didn't want me to see where he was taking me. But why would he not want me to look at his truck? What could he not want me to see?

I was naked, except for the shorts on my head, sitting on the blanket with my knees drawn up close to my chest. My hands were still tied behind my back so I used my knee to; disobediently push the shorts up just enough to see what he was doing. I saw him go to the passenger's side of the truck where it looked like he picked something up off the floor. And that's when I really started to panic. I remembered what was on the floor of the passenger side because for twenty minutes earlier that day that is all I stared at. The only things on the floor were shotgun shells!

Next, he went around to the back of the truck and it looked like he was getting something out of the back. He was getting a gun! He must be! What else could he have been getting? Of course later, when he recounted the events of this afternoon to the police, he would claim that he was getting me some water. What a gentleman, huh? Why wouldn't he be getting me water?!? Only a complete psychopath would kidnap someone by running her down with his truck, brutally rape her and NOT get her some water!

That was the moment when I knew the only hope I had was gone. He was going to kill me! Up until that point, I was holding onto the chance that he might let me go. I knew my chances were slim but, what can I say, I'm an optimist.

Would someone hear the shotgun go off? If they did, would it matter? In a small farming community how uncommon is it to hear a shotgun go off? Was he going to bury me in the woods?

Fight or flight?!? There was that feeling again but this time it was different. He was twenty feet away from me with his head in the back of the truck. Would I be able to outrun him? I knew I was fast. I could outrun this man any day but today I would be running barefoot through the woods, while he had shoes on. I, also, was in the middle of the woods. If I ran in the wrong direction I would just run deeper into the woods and he would surely catch me.

I figured I had two choices. I could run for it and hope I ran in the right direction or I could just accept the fact that I was going to die and prepare myself. In those few moments I had while he was "getting me a glass of water", I sighed to myself, "God please help me!"

I wasn't asking Him for help to get me out of this situation because I believed it wasn't possible. And after all, I wasn't too sure God would listen to me anyway. I had turned my back on Him a long time ago. If anything, I was just crying out in desperation; asking for the strength to endure what was surely coming next. I was going to die!

It was at that moment that I clearly heard someone tell me to stand up; to turn around, and to run. I remembered being startled for a second and thinking, "Did I just hear that?" I know this must sound crazy but I believe it was God giving me guidance; telling me what to do. I hadn't spoken to God in a very long time, so I didn't understand why He would be speaking to me at that moment but I decided to listen. What was my other option?

I used my knees to push my shorts off of my head. I turned completely around and I ran into the woods. I didn't look back but I knew he was there. I could hear him yelling at me to stop.

The trees and the bushes were lashing at my face and body, breaking my skin open but I couldn't feel it. I just kept running. When I think about this I'm right there again. I can feel the adrenaline. I can see the trees and the forest floor in front of me. He chased me to the end of the forest but he stopped when I broke through the tree line.

Now I was in a field. I saw a road and a house about two hundred yards away. I ran toward the house, naked and bleeding. I couldn't cover myself because my hands were still tied behind my back. I must have been screaming because a man came outside and was staring at me.

Who was this man? Why was his house so close to the place I had been taken? Did he know my attacker? Could this be his brother? These thoughts were racing through my head as I continued to run toward him.

"Each heart knows its own bitterness, and no one can share its joy."
Proverbs 14: 10

My Quiet Comfort

By the time I reached the house there was a woman running toward me with a blanket. At some point, one of them must have untied my hands and wrapped the blanket around me. Whether they knew my captor or not, they helped me, because the next thing I remember are police officers. There were people everywhere asking me questions and looking at me with sympathetic eyes. There was the man and the woman, the police officers, the paramedics, and, what felt like, every neighbor, all staring at me. I tried to sit somewhere out of the way where I wasn't the center of attention, but I knew that was impossible.

I WAS THE CENTER OF ATTENTION!

I wanted to pull the blanket over my head and disappear. Maybe I did. I don't remember. A woman

told me about this girl who was there. She said she
went to my school and that her name was Tina.
Maybe she thought that someone my own age
would make me feel better somehow. I didn't know
Tina but I recognized her from school. She was a
quiet girl who I had seen in the hallways between
classes.

For some reason, just being near her was
comforting. We didn't talk to each other much. In
fact, I don't remember saying anything to her at
all. She just stood near me, quietly protecting me
from all the strangers that wouldn't stop talking
and staring.

Her presence meant more to me than I probably
realized at the time. She represented everything
that was "normal" to me.

To this day, when I think about Tina I feel safe
and comforted. I saw her in the hallway at school a
few weeks later. Our eyes met and we just smiled
and nodded at each other.

I've never told you but I will always be grateful
to you, Tina, for your quiet comfort. Thank you.

"The eye that now sees me will see me no longer; you will look for me, but I will be no more."

Job 7: 8

Dream Walking

I was taken to the hospital where I was given the "once over" by the doctors and nurses. I was given the controversial "morning-after" pill, which was virtually unheard of in 1991. Then, I was given the "once over" by the police officers, where I was asked to recall every little detail I could remember. I told them about his tattoo, his brother, the little girl, the shotgun shells, his wife and kid. Then, I was given the "once over" by the sketch artist. They said I gave a really good description, except I told them he was in his 40's but he was only 29.

He looked pretty bad for 29!

Then, I was given the "once over" by the rape counselor. I told her I was fine. I would be fine...blah, blah, blah. I can be a great liar when it comes to my feelings.

I must have told my story about a dozen times that day but I don't remember it coming out of my mouth. It's strange that I can remember my attack so vividly but I have very little memory of my rescue. It's as if my mind knew I was finally safe so it shut down. I can recall bits and pieces of that Sunday's aftermath but that's it. I remember being embarrassed because everyone was paying so much attention to me. I wanted them to stop talking about it. I wanted them to stop looking at me. I didn't want to be comforted. I wanted to forget about it, which is why I went to school on Monday.

"That God would be willing to crush me, to let loose His hand and cut me off!"

Job 6: 9

Assumptions

I like to deal with my problems by pretending nothing's wrong, which is why I returned to school on Monday. I was so desperate for my life to return to normal. The news couldn't release my name because I was a minor so I assumed that I was quite anonymous.

Have you ever heard that saying about assuming? Don't assume anything because you'll make an ASS out of U and ME, right? What I'm trying to say is, as anyone who comes from a small town already knows, is no one is ever anonymous.

Everyone was surprised to see me in school so soon but they were cool about it. I pretended it didn't happen and so did they...for the most part. There was probably a lot of talk when I wasn't in the room but as long as I didn't hear it, I didn't care. Only my closest friends were allowed to question me and I could tell that even they were uncomfortable around me.

Everyone knew what happened to me and no one knew how to treat me. They didn't know what to say. I could feel their eyes on me at all times. "That's the girl who was raped!" I was so embarrassed. I was afraid that someone was going to break the unwritten rule and ask me about it. I couldn't look anyone in the eye because in their eyes I could see their pity. I was a freak! I hated being around people that knew what happened to me because, in my eyes, they were all picturing me being raped!

"My soul is weary with sorrow; strengthen me according to Your word."

Psalm 119:28

Sleeping With the Enemy

-Renee's Story

April 28th, 1991 was a Sunday. Jim came home from work around one in the afternoon changed his clothes and headed back out the door. I had been with the baby all morning and needed a break, so I handed her to Jim and said "Please take her with you. I just need a few minutes of peace" He was agitated but he took her and left. When he came back he insisted we take a drive to a buddy's house to pick up some tools he had lent to him. I wanted to stay home but he insisted that I go along. This seemed really odd to me at the time, he never wanted to spend time with me. Come to find out, this friend lived a good two hours away.

The conversation in the car was very strange. It was as if we were really friends again, like he really cared about me, almost as if he was sorry for the way he had been treating me. He had me convinced that he had had a change of heart and things would be good with us. We got home late that night, his friend wasn't home. You know how hindsight is 20/20, well, I bet there was no friend, and I think we drove around for hours to avoid being at home so he wouldn't get caught for what he had done to you.

Part of the conversation we had, centered on the massive tornados that had happened in the Midwest and how there was so much work for carpenters. He told me he was seriously thinking about heading out there to work. He could make tons of money and would probably be there six months and would send money home every week.

The next morning I went out to get the paper from the paper box and it wasn't there. I called the newspaper and asked why it was so late. They said it had been delivered. I called the paper carrier, no answer. I was putting on my shoes to go down to the store and get a paper when Jim said, "No, I'll get it." and went for me. I didn't think anything of it. When he got back he said there were no more papers, they had all been sold. Well, it was a little annoying but really no big deal, just a bit odd. Again, I didn't think much about it at the time.

My sister called later that day and told me of an article that had been in the paper. She wanted to be sure I had seen it. I hadn't. There was a rapist loose in our small town community. Everyone was talking about it. She read me the article and they were looking for a man with similar tattoos to the ones Jim had. I remember that night before bed talking to Jim telling him about the article in the paper. I was holding his arm in my hand and saying, "You need to keep these tattoos covered because the guy they are looking for has tattoos just like these except his are a little different."

It had been a wet spring and for some reason or another we had the skirting around our trailer opened up during the day. I usually went out and closed it at night, but that night I was afraid so I asked Jim to go out and close it. And I said "We'd better start locking the doors too", yes I was one who NEVER locked her doors, ever. It never occurred to me that I was locking myself inside with the very man the police were looking for.

The next day Jim became sure that heading out west was the right thing to do, he could make lots of money and he'd be leaving the next day. This just blew my mind. Part of me knew he was leaving me and this was just an excuse, but part of me was relieved. He continued to tell me he loved me but the night before he left he fell promptly asleep. If I was leaving my spouse for six months or more and I truly loved them, sleep would be the last thing on my mind the night before I left.

In the morning when he left he told me he was going to go to see his mom before he headed out west. It was a very difficult morning, I cried continually. The first thing I did was call my friend that use to work in law enforcement and tell him that something was up. I asked if he had found anything out and he told me he would call me back.

The next thing I knew my house had several police cars and investigators all over it. There were tons of investigators and cops, everyone asking the same questions and no one answering any of my questions. Why there were so many police cars for what I thought was probably stolen merchandise? It didn't add up. The one really bizarre thing I remember from this day is the property manager of the park called in the middle of the mayhem and told me "Your guests have to park in your driveway. They cannot park on the roadway." He was very nasty about it, so I told him if he'd like to come over and explain that to the police he could be my guest. He never showed up.

My dad came over, he was able to get out of the investigator that they wanted him for the rape of a local girl. They searched my home, they took things, they went through every closet, every drawer of my home. They even looked through the diaper pail.

I kept telling them that he couldn't be the man they were looking for. He was with me from one o'clock on, all day, and all night. It was impossible. I didn't believe them. I never did. I was formulating in my mind how to find a good lawyer who could help him and how I would pay for it. I had worked myself out of a job the previous January and was collecting unemployment.

That was one very long, very emotional, very frustrating day. The next day I had to face my neighbor Cynthia and tell her what he had been arrested for. Jim would occasionally watch her infant daughter Alyssa for her, while she was working. Alyssa was Tara's age. Cynthia took her immediately to the doctors to be checked. That was a wakeup call for me. I became hysterical and called my pediatrician as well. Both girls checked out all right. Thank God!

"For our light and momentary troubles are achieving for us an eternal glory that far outweighs them all."

2 Corinthians 4: 17

His Capture

It didn't take long for the police to catch him. They had him in custody by May 1st. I found out fifteen years later (that's how long it took me to start asking questions) that his wife played a key role in his capture. That must have been really hard for her to learn what her husband was capable of. Then again, maybe she already knew.

Either way, I find it all very frightening. You think you know someone. You marry them and spend years with them and then one day you find out he's a viscous animal who's capable of unspeakable things. Can you even imagine? They had a daughter together too. She would be twenty or twenty one years old now. I often wonder if she knows what her father is in prison for. She was so young when it happened. I heard her mother remarried and that her new step-father legally adopted her. I think that's nice. I hope he is a good father to her.

Some days I think about finding his ex-wife just so I can give her a great, big hug and tell her how much I appreciate what she did. But I don't because that would be weird. I mean, what would I say to her? How would I introduce myself?

I was told that he has threatened to kill her when he gets out because she helped them capture him. Apparently, everyone is accountable...except for himself.

"Remember, O God, that my life is but a breath; my eyes will never see happiness again."

Job 7: 7

The Line Up

Once they had him in custody, I had to go down and identify him in a line-up. That was horrifying! I had never had to do anything like that before. I'd only seen line ups in movies. In the movies it seems like the victim looks at the line up for such a long time. They look at each possible suspect with such scrutiny and concentration because they're not sure which one is the right one. They don't want to make a mistake and choose the wrong one.

In my case, I barely had to look at the other "suspects." They were barely in position before I identified my attacker. I was 100% positive. How could I forget that face?!?

Once I'd seen him I looked away. I couldn't look at him even though I knew he couldn't see me. I was afraid he was going to come through the glass and get me. We were so close to each other. I started feeling boxed in and anxious to get out of there. I was nauseous just knowing I was in the same building as he was, sharing his air once again.

"If only my anguish could be weighed, and all my misery be placed on the scales! It would surely outweigh the sand of the sea..."

Job 6: 2 - 3

The Grand Jury

I'm not sure how much time had passed before I had to go in front of the grand jury, maybe a week or two. In case you don't know what the grand jury is, it's a room full of complete strangers that are there to listen to you tell your story. That was a horrible, HORRIBLE day!

Policemen came to my school to pick me up and take me to the courthouse. The principal let me take three friends with me, which I thought was cool of him. I chose Danyelle, Sarah and Mark. It turned out Mark wasn't completely repulsed by what had happened to me. We started dating and we stayed together for a little over two years. It was pretty rocky but I'll tell you more about that later.

So, the four of us rode in the police car down to the courthouse. They gave us a room to sit in but the three of them were pretty much by themselves most of the time while I was chauffeured from room to room telling my story to complete strangers...again. I'm sure my friends were terribly bored but I appreciated their "sacrifice" so much.

I was not looking forward to telling my story to the grand jury. Up until then, I only had to tell individuals. Now I had to tell about a dozen or so strangers at once. That was not going to be easy. When I got into the room there was a small group of people sitting in a classroom-like arrangement facing a lone stool that was positioned at the front of the room. I was expected to sit on the stool and repeat my story to them. (GULP!)

I sat on the stool but nothing came out of my mouth. They tried to coax it out of me with kind words but it didn't work. I just sat there and cried for them. Finally, someone asked me if it would be easier for me to share if they turned off the lights. Of course, I knew that turning off the lights wouldn't make me invisible but if I couldn't see their faces it seemed like it would be easier for me to talk to them. I said yes. They turned off the lights and I took it one step further by turning around on the stool so I wasn't facing them. I got through my story that way.

"How long will you defend the unjust, and show partiality of the wicked?"

Psalms 82: 2

His Sentence

My attacker ended up pleading guilty, which meant my case didn't have to go to trial. I was done feeling forced to tell my story! I didn't have to go to anymore offices to identify an item they'd found or describe in detail what he had done to me anymore. It was an immediate relief, followed shortly thereafter by the realization that because he pleaded guilty he only received fifteen to twenty five years with the chance of parole in eleven.

His sentence seemed light to me, but I was told that it was the harshest sentence he could have received in the state of New York. Can you believe that?!? Getting caught with marijuana can get you a harsher sentence than kidnap, rape and intent to murder?!? Where's the justice in that? And apparently, no one had the foresight to have me apply for an order of protection against my attacker. That was the only time I could've been granted one. One might think of a restraining order as unnecessary since he would be behind bars for at least eleven years but listen to this...On April 28, 2002 he had his first parole hearing. He was denied. Since then, he's had a hearing every year but has ALWAYS been denied. Do you want to know why?

In his eighteen years behind bars, he has threatened to kill the judge who sentenced him, the District Attorney who prosecuted him, his ex-wife who turned him in, and a few guards who have "crossed" him. He has also written me letters, which have been intercepted by the police; therefore I have never read them. I could have read them, but I had no interest in what he had to say. What could a man who has taken absolutely no responsibility for any of the harm he's caused, have to say to the girl he brutalized?

He has also tried to obtain photographs of me from my town's library by pretending to be my step-brother. And he's done all of this from the confines of his maximum security prison cell. Luckily, the librarian had the intuition to be suspicious. I guess it pays to come from a small town.

Nobody wants this guy back on the street. They KNOW he is not rehabilitated. They KNOW he is still dangerous, but their hands are tied by the judicial system. They can only hold him for so long. He WILL be released on April 28, 2011, regardless of their best efforts. He will be let loose on some unsuspecting town somewhere in the state of New York.

Their description of him, and I quote, "He's just plain evil!"

"You may ask me for anything in my name, and I will do it."

John 14:14

Answered Prayers

-Renee's story

This is a very dark and confusing area of my life. One moment I would catch myself wondering how I was going to make it till Jim was back home with us, the next moment I would be thanking God for taking him away.

The nights were always the hardest. I would put Tara to bed and then take the monitor with me and do laps around our park. I could always see our house, there was no way I'd go anywhere where I couldn't see my door. I would walk for hours checking in on her every lap. I would walk until I was so exhausted I couldn't take one more step, and yet sleep wouldn't come.

I learned a very valuable lesson, when you ask God for something, be prepared that He will answer your prayers with a yes. I had asked God to take

Jim away. I needed some peace in my life, some rest, but I didn't ask for that, I asked for him to go away. I had never had any major prayer answered in the affirmative before. Sure, I got an "A" on a test, or I got to an appointment on time, but when I think about God answering my prayers back then it was always "Not yet" or "In my time" or, "You're not ready yet", it was never "YES, sure thing, right away, how'd I do? Was that quick enough?"

I learned to be very careful about what I prayed for. I have never prayed the same since.

"If I have sinned, what have I done to You, O watcher of men? Why have You made me Your target? Have I become a burden to You?"

Job 7: 20

Questioning God

I refused to accept what had happened to me. I wouldn't talk about it, and when someone would bring it up, I answered their questions without emotion. I met their eyes with what I thought was unquestionable strength. I dismissed their concerns as trivial. I refused to admit that this had ruined me...but it had. I was broken! I spent a lot of my time pretending.

I kept myself busy with school and friends. I joined a lot of clubs and groups in the hopes of keeping my mind off of what happened to me. I became a member of chorus, select chorus, French club, SADD and cheerleading. I was the president of SADD, which was pretty ridiculous if you knew me back then. I did anything to keep my mind off of what had happened to me. This worked until nighttime when my friends had to go home and I was alone. I no longer appreciated the silence. Silence was painful.

I was not a particularly religious person. As I told you before, I only occasionally went to church, because it was convenient. Something that helped me pass the time and get me out of my mother's hair. But I hadn't been to church since my 7th grade year when I was thirteen. When I was nine I did become a Christian. I prayed and asked for forgiveness and asked Jesus to come into my heart. At that moment, I believed in God with all of my heart. But, just believing wasn't good enough.

As I grew up, I turned my back on God. By the time I was seventeen, I was indulging in ALL of the seven deadly sins. I was smoking cigarettes, drinking alcohol and having sex. All of my friends were. I was heavily influenced by peer pressure and I had no positive influences in my life. I had turned my back on God for so long, but I couldn't shake the feeling that He had spoken to me in the forest that day. If it wasn't for that voice in my head, I don't think I would have made it out of the woods.

Did that mean that God had saved me? If that were true then didn't that also mean that He had let it happen?

In my broken mind, I began questioning God. Why didn't He stop that man? Didn't He love me? Was He punishing me? When I couldn't find the answers to my questions, I began questioning His very existence. Did God really exist? If there was a

God, would He allow His children to be in such pain? Abuse, divorce, death, war, betrayal, disease? These things wouldn't exist, couldn't exist if there was a God...could they?!?

"Love is patient, love is kind. It does not envy, it does not boast, it is not proud. It is not rude, it is not self-seeking, it is not easily angered, it keeps no record of wrongs. Love does not delight in evil but rejoices with the truth. It always protects, always trusts, always hopes, and always perseveres."

1 Corinthians 13:4-7

Tainted Love

Mark and I were soon spending a lot of time together. He was wonderful and supportive. Everything a girl could ask for in a boyfriend. There was nothing we didn't share or talk about, with one exception...my rape. I fell in love with him easily, but that didn't stop me from ripping his heart out and stomping it into a million pieces more than once.

Our relationship lasted a little over two years, and for the most part, he kept me grounded. When I was with him, which was most of the time, everything was great. The problems started when I wasn't with him. I realize now, after having more time to think about it, that I had incredibly low self-esteem. I had low self-esteem even before "the incident", but now I felt utterly untouchable.

I was already an occasional drinker and so were most of my friends, so when I started drinking more often, it went unnoticed. Every weekend became a party that Mark couldn't always attend, and as they say...boys will be boys. I couldn't blame them for trying. It amazed me each and every time some boy showed a little interest in me. Had they not heard that I was tainted? Most of them didn't try for fear of Mark. He was a big, well respected football player. Not too many boys were stupid enough to mess with him, but there were a few. There were three to be exact. And, Mark just kept taking me back.

I'm not sure why I had such a hard time remaining faithful to such a wonderful person. To this day, I worry that maybe I ruined his vision of love. Does he have a hard time trusting others because of me? Does he have a hard time staying faithful now because of what I taught him? I used to think that he was my soul mate and against all odds we would end up together. But I no longer think that because I married my soul mate. My intelligent, stubborn, beautiful, egotistical, wonderful, annoying, honorable, vain, perfect for me soul mate.

"The Lord gave and the Lord has taken away; may the name of the Lord be praised."

Job 1: 21

Are you there God?

Mark's parents were Christians and just all around amazing people. They were so generous. They welcomed all three of their sons' friends into their home and made them feel like they were a part of their family. They even fed them. They must have spent a small fortune on food. When they saw how serious their son and I were becoming they started trying to get us to go to church with them. They talked about God with us every chance they had. When I graduated from high school they bought me a Bible.

At that point in my life, I had given up on God. I had convinced myself that if He did exist, then He wouldn't have let that man hurt me. Mark, on the other hand, DID believe in God and it was for that reason that I agreed to go to church with him...once. Nothing miraculous happened. I wasn't "moved by the spirit" or anything, but something weird did happen. I met Mark's grandmother.

Mark's grandmother just so happened to be the very same woman who prayed with me when I was nine years old and asked Jesus to forgive me for my sins. Was this a coincidence? If it was, it was pretty weird. I couldn't help but think that maybe God was tapping me on my shoulder and reminding me that He was still there. That He did exist and He still loved me. After thinking this I realized, maybe I hadn't completely given up on God. If I had truly believed that God didn't exist then I wouldn't have considered these things.

When Mark and I broke up after two years of being together, it was a very sad time in my life. Not only was our relationship over but my relationship with his family was over as well. I loved them like they were my own family. They were my positive influence. What would happen now?

"What strength do I have, that I should still hope? What prospects, that I should be patient?"

Job 6: 11

My Journal

I have kept a journal since I was fifteen years old, and amazingly, I found the journal from the time of my rape. There are entries up until April 27 but then nothing until four months later. I read through my journal and I found nothing at all about my rape, until I got to September 28, 1992. It was followed by a poem that was written by my brother.

I think you should know that I gave my journal a name. It made me feel like I was writing to an actual person instead of to myself. My journal's name was Alice Cooper, but I called her Allie for short. I guess I was a little bizarre, huh?

Allie,   Sept.28, 1992

Finally, after one year and five months (to the day) I've decided to get counseling for my accident. I called the Crime Victim Assistance Center and set up an appointment for October 8 at 11:00. I really need help, too. I don't know if I'm up for it but I've got to be helped somehow. I'm a basket case. Not one day goes by when I don't think about what happened at least 50xs. I'm not exaggerating!

Today, in my criminal justice class, we were talking about crime victims and the issue of "was a rape victim asking for it if she was wearing a mini skirt" came up. I tried to give my opinion. I finally got everything out that I was trying to say but just in the nick of time. I almost burst into tears. My face turned so red. Everyone had to see it. I was so red! I started sweating and my voice started cracking. And since I was talking, the whole class was looking at me. I was so embarrassed! Anyway, that's when I decided "I need help!" I'll tell you how it goes once I feel up to it.

No one sees me as I am.

No one hears my cries for help.

My aura hides my plea for death.

Through laughter my heart plays charades.

No one sees me as I am.

No one hears my cries for help.

As I beg to see my life through the distorted
mirrors eyes.

I see myself struggle through another day.

Reality's walls close in around me.

No one sees me as I am.

No one hears my cries for help.

How much longer can I play this game?

I never went to the counseling appointment.

"But now, Lord, what do I look for? My hope is in You."

Psalm 39:7

God's Subtle Miracles

-Renee's Story

Tara was a great kid. She never woke up at night. She never climbed out of her crib. She was potty trained at eighteen months. This was because she was in cloth diapers and hated being wet. She had a normal vocabulary of about fifty or so words and was putting two word sentences together. Simple things like "mama up", "mama baba", that was her sippy cup, "mama be", when she wanted her blanket.

I went to the court house the day Jim stood before the Judge and admitted that he was guilty. That was the day that erased all doubt from my mind. Up until then I had gone back and forth in my head between believing him and not believing him. Up until that day he assured me he hadn't done anything. They had the wrong person. He had given me the girl's name and asked me to call and talk to her and try to get her to recant. There had always been that one small part of me that held out hope that I couldn't have been fooled that easily.

I don't know if he knew I was in the courtroom that day. I just remember sitting near the back sobbing silently. Tears were pouring down my face. I don't know how long I sat there but I do know that I didn't know any of the people on the stand or in the courtroom when I left.

I needed someone to hear me, to care. I called the crime victims assistance center. They had me come right in. I told my story. But just like all of my "friends" I felt like they asked questions because they wanted to know more. Not because they wanted to help or even could. Its funny how many friends disappear during times of crisis. Nobody just listened and cared.

One night I was so depressed. I had been to see my doctor and he had prescribed Paxil for my depression. I had been taking it for a while but nothing was helping. I was in such a dark place. I put Tara to bed in her crib at 7:30 or so, it was just starting to get dark. I picked up the monitor and started doing laps. By 10:00 it was raining. It was that light misty rain that doesn't really bother you; you can be out in it not really getting too wet. But I had been out in it for hours and by midnight I was drenched. I finally went inside and sat at the window and stared out of it. I could see the headlights of the cars and trucks on the interstate from where I sat, rocking back and forth, back and forth. It was mesmerizing, comforting, and peaceful. Those lights, they were calling me.

My mom was coming over in the morning. Tara never got out of her crib until I took her out. She would be safe until my mom got here. I could go for a walk, into the lights. Out of the hell that was my life.

I sat and rocked and prayed for hours. Not the kind of prayers I used to pray. This time I was asking forgiveness for what I was about to do. Asking that God protect Tara and find her someone to take care of her and raise her to be a wonderful person. As I sat there I felt a tiny little hand on my hand; then a leg on my leg. Then a little tiny voice said "mama up". I reached down and picked her up. She sat kneeling facing towards me. I said "What are you doing up?" She reached out her little hand and wiped my tears and said "Mama, I love you" and gave me the biggest hug. That was exactly what I needed. Someone to care. Someone to love me for me. No one who would judge me. I held her right there in my arms the rest of the night. God had rescued me again.

"Pride goeth before destruction, a haughty spirit before a fall."

Proverbs 16: 18

Downward Spiral

My downward spiral began the summer of 1993, when Mark joined the Army. After he left, I quickly came unraveled. Once he was gone, I had no one to answer to. I still lived at home with my mother, but I came and went as I pleased. She seemed content with NOT knowing what I was doing and so was I. I had a job, so I had money. I had a car, so I had freedom.

It was at this time that I discovered drugs...I mean, REALLY discovered drugs. Every Friday night became Acid Friday. Every Friday for the next three months, I was either drunk or "tripping on acid". The once President of SADD became a really good drunk driver...something I'm not proud of, but then again, I'm not very proud of a lot of things I've done in my past. The only time I was sober was when I went to work and I couldn't get out of there fast enough! I loved the fantasy world I had created for myself, but as long as I was around people who knew what had happened to me, I didn't feel free.

So I moved in with a very close friend of mine who I had been friends with since I was twelve years old. Her name was Leigh and she lived in a different state where I could start over again, but that's not exactly what happened. I just created a new fantasy world for myself. In this new world I discovered all kinds of new drugs. They were everywhere and I tried them all, but my drug of choice was cocaine. I would stay awake for days on end with the help of cocaine. When my nose would start bleeding I would just wipe it up and move on. When I had a cold I would use nasal spray so I could snuff up my beloved drug of choice.

If all of this weren't destructive enough, and against Leigh's advice, I took a job as a topless dancer, where I was NOT allowed to deny a drink bought for me by a customer. I was drunk the first night I danced. Me and two other of my friends decided it would be easy money. I thought it would be hard for me to expose myself in that way after what I had been through, but instead it empowered me. It was a way for me to control the men around me the way he had controlled me. There was nothing these men wouldn't give a woman who was willing to take their clothes off for them. There was nothing we were denied...alcohol, drugs, concert tickets, boob jobs, college tuition, jewelry, clothing. We didn't even have to have sex with them...and I DIDN'T. They still gave willingly.

But I was kidding myself. They didn't want me. They didn't care about me. They were in their own fantasy world. Of course, I couldn't see that. I felt loved and admired. I was making at least $1500 a week, but I couldn't snap back into reality long enough to pay my bills. My car was repossessed one night, while I was onstage.

My car was my lifeline. I practically lived in it...literally. Technically I still lived with Leigh but most nights I ended up passed out in my car. Without my car, I couldn't sleep in it or make the forty minute commute back to Leigh's house. It was for this reason that I hopped a bus back to my mommy. If I had stayed I don't think I would've survived much longer. I had hit rock bottom. I had no money to my name even though I was making plenty. I was so strung out I didn't even know what day it was.

Having my car repossessed was a blessing in disguise. It changed the course of my life.

"Hatred stirs up dissension, but love covers over all wrongs."

Proverbs 10: 12

Back to Reality

Now what was I supposed to do? I had no car. I had no job. I had alienated myself from everyone except my drug connections, and they weren't as excited to see me as they were when I had money. My fantasy world came crashing down.

My mom let me crash on her couch until I got a job and a place of my own. I immediately started looking for a job but I wasn't qualified for much. I knew I could probably get my old job back if I begged but that was the last thing I wanted to do. I did NOT leave on good terms. If you asked me, I quit, but if you asked them, I was fired.

With the exception of my boss, who I think had a crush on me, everyone else HATED me. One of my ex-boyfriends, my future husband, and even my brother, who were my supervisors, HATED me!

I didn't blame them. I had "screwed them over" so many times.

After three weeks of job searching and rejection, I swallowed my pride and went to see my old boss, Dave. I didn't expect a warm welcome when I walked in there, but he seemed genuinely happy to see me. He hired me back after I assured him I was a changed girl. I like to think that Dave saw my regret and my potential, but it was probably the skimpy outfit I was wearing, because not only did he hire me back, he gave me a pretty hefty raise. Maybe he felt sorry for me. Maybe he was just one of those really nice guys. Don't get me wrong. I was extremely appreciative. I could definitely use all the money I could get, but I was pretty sure that I got the job and the raise because of the way I looked.

I know this must sound strange coming from someone who gets things because of the way they look, but it doesn't help your self-esteem. You think it would, but in the long run it just teaches you that you don't have to be smart or try hard to get what you want. You just have to look good and when you stop looking good you have nothing left. You haven't learned any other way.

At the time, I didn't care. I had a job making more than I expected to be making. The raise did NOT help my popularity though and my co-workers did NOT make the transition into reality easy.

"Whatever your hand finds to do, do it with all your might."

Eccleciastes 9: 10

Adjusting

I found an apartment within walking distance to my work. It allowed me to pay by the week, which was best since I was so terrible with money. As soon as I cashed my paycheck I would go pay my rent. I was bringing home $180 a week and $80 of it went toward my rent. Remember this was the early 90's when minimum wage was like, $4.25 or something like that.

I quickly and surprisingly, became one of the best workers there...at least in my opinion. I found working hard came easy to me. I was available to work whenever I was needed and I worked as many hours as I possibly could, which was only forty hours a week. My co-workers stopped being mean to me and started treating me with...respect?!? Were they treating me with respect?

I slowly became accepted and I began to enjoy working there. It felt good to be respected and appreciated. It became my new "drug." I still struggled with being accepted by the older women that I worked with, but at least they were civil. Even my brother, who was one of my supervisors, gave me a second chance. We were getting along again.

I was bound and determined to prove to all of these people that I deserved this second chance AND that raise. I wanted to be taken seriously.

"And we know that in all things God works for the good of those who love Him, who have been called according to His purpose."

Romans 8: 28

Go Figure!

By August of that year, I was doing pretty well. I had a job and a place to live. I was paying my bills but more importantly, I was sober. For the past two months, I had been completely sober. I stopped hanging out with my old friends because they didn't understand why I wanted to be sober. So I made new friends.

One of my new friends was someone I had known for a few years. His name was Martin and he was unlike anyone I had ever met. He grew up extremely poor. He spent most of his childhood without electricity or running water. He got his first job at age eight picking apples at an apple orchard. During the winter, he worked on a Christmas tree farm. He worked both jobs until he was fourteen, when he got a job as a janitor at an elementary school. He was a Christian. His mother was a reverend. He graduated from a Christian high school and a Christian college. He had NEVER had a drink of alcohol or used any kind of illegal drug in his life...EVER! He didn't understand why anyone would want to lose control of themselves in that way. He was smart, serious, fun, hardworking, responsible, shy, cute, and I had a crush on him.

For about a month, I thought of ways to get him to like me back. I found ways to hang out with him outside of work. I flirted with him in my usual manner but he didn't seem interested in me in that way. I couldn't blame him. Compared to him, I felt like trash.

We had become pretty good friends and because of that he knew quite a lot about me...except what had happened to me three years earlier. He knew about my drug use, my drinking, my promiscuity, my topless dancing. Why would someone like him be interested in someone like me? I decided to take a different approach to this situation.

We worked with this girl named Jenn, who loved to gossip. A girl that gossiped? I know, weird right? I decided to "let it slip" that I had a crush on Martin. It would be quite the scandalous rumor...the ex topless dancer falling for her Christian supervisor. She was sure to tell him...and she did. Within a few days everybody had heard the rumor. All I had to do was confirm it. I played coy. "Oh no! He knows I like him?!? How embarrassing! What did he say?"

She ate it up. I would "let slip" something I wanted Martin to know and she would run over and tell him the first chance she got. Of course, this little game worked both ways. It wasn't long before I knew he was interested in me as well. Go figure!

One day, Martin came to my apartment. I invited him in and we sat down on the couch. He told me he couldn't stay long because he was on his way to work, but he wanted to know if I would go on a date with him this weekend. Of course I said yes.

I was giddy and nervous at the same time. This would be my first actual date.

"Above all, love each other deeply, because love covers over a multitude of sins."

1 Peter 4: 8

Our First Date

The big day was set for August 18th. Martin took me to a really expensive restaurant. One of those places that doesn't serve anything that sounds appetizing, if you know what I mean. There was pan seared prawn, truffled risotto, baby octopus, quail and golden raisin. He could've saved money by taking me somewhere less expensive and I would've been just as impressed. I wouldn't have known the difference. I was so uncultured. Up until that moment, a five star restaurant was Red Lobster.

Not only did he take me to this beautiful restaurant that was situated on a lake with amazing views, it took us about an hour to drive there. After dinner, he took me to a beautiful park where we walked and talked and watched the sunset together. Again...another first. Twenty years old and I had never watched the sunset.

The entire evening was beautiful but I felt so uncomfortable the whole time. It felt strange having someone treat me this way. I had never been respected enough to be treated like a lady. He seemed interested in what I was saying and he kept looking at me funny. Kind of glassy eyed and dreamy. The kind of look someone gives you when they want to tell you something but they're not supposed to, so they just smile at you, hoping you'll figure it out on your own. I don't know. It was weird.

I suddenly didn't know how to talk to him. We had been friends for almost three years. I'd never had a hard time talking to him before. Up until this date, I was totally at ease with Martin. What had changed in the hours leading up to this moment?

At the end of the night, when we said our 'goodnights', I could tell he wasn't going to kiss me. A good ol' Christian boy like that? That would be improper. But this was me, after all. So I stood there looking into his eyes with a devilish grin on my face for a few moments. I batted my baby blues a few times. Then, I leaned a little closer to him, but not too close. I was waiting to see if he would lean closer. If he didn't I would just hug him and pretend that's all I was going to do in the first place, but wouldn't you know it...he leaned in and kissed me...on my cheek.

It was very sweet, even if it was only on my cheek. Maybe he was worried about contracting an infectious disease from the ex-stripper. I don't know, but instead of feeling rejected, I felt even more respected. It was at that moment that I realized I had fallen in love with Martin. Would he be able to love me back?

"Now faith is being sure of what we hope for and certain of what we do not see."

Hebrews 11: 1

Reverend Jane

Martin and I began spending all of our time together. If we weren't at work then we were somewhere with each other. We were inseparable. One night, we were hanging out at my apartment. We had lost track of time and it was really late so Martin stayed the night. Then, he stayed over the next night, and the next night, and the next night. Before I knew it, he had moved in with me. He still had his own apartment but he only went there when he needed to get something. We gradually moved in together. We were happy about it, too.

His mother, on the other hand, was NOT! She was a reverend after all and her baby boy was "living in sin." I'm not sure how much of her feelings she revealed to me but she wasn't exactly the 'suffer in silence' type. She made it clear that she disapproved of our 'shackin' up.'

When she saw that her disapproval wasn't going to influence us, she must have decided that Jesus was the only one that could. She started inviting us to church every Sunday morning, every Sunday evening, and every Wednesday evening. She invited us to church picnics, concerts, bowling parties, roller skating parties. You name it, if it involved church she tried to get us to go. She talked about church and Jesus so much that it had the opposite effect on me than what she was hoping for.

It wasn't until 1999 that she finally 'broke' me. Five years of constant nagging. She was always opinionated, always persistent, always spiritual...yet, she was also always accepting, always loving, and always kind. She might have been annoyingly persistent, but things might have been a lot different if she had been more apathetic.

It was because of her that I finally went to church. It was because of her influence that I finally realized that God was there, He had always been there. I just chose not to pay attention to Him. I am so grateful to her for never giving up on me.

Thank you, Jane. I love you.

"Though You have made me troubles, many and bitter, You will restore my life again."

Psalm 71: 20

Coming out of the Dark

Adjusting to life as a fulltime, live-in girlfriend who no longer had the freedom to come and go as she pleased without first consulting another person was easy...at first. Don't get me wrong, I loved Martin and I loved being his girlfriend. I even dreamed of someday becoming Mrs. Martin. What I had trouble with was being intimate with Martin. Not physically intimate but emotionally intimate. I think a lot of the problem stemmed from the fact that I didn't know myself very well, so how was I going to explain my feelings to someone else.

See, I had put up a front to the world. I was the girl who didn't care what you thought of me. I was the "fun girl" who hid her pain behind her sense of humor. I certainly wasn't the fragile girl who had a hard time functioning. The girl who cried inside every time something triggered her memory. The girl who just wanted to curl up in a ball and hide. No, I was strong and secure! That's who Martin fell in love with.

Keeping up the facade was a fulltime job and I could only do it up for so long. That's why I didn't have a lot of friends. As a matter of fact, I didn't have any close friends in my life. I had managed to push them all away. Even Leigh, who had been like a sister to me since we were twelve years-old had been somewhat pushed away. I felt like I had to replace them before they caught on to my scam. The same thing happened in my past relationships. I would eventually get tired of hiding and would subconsciously sabotage the relationship. I couldn't possibly let them in on my little secret. I couldn't let them know that I was broken without hope of recovery. Then they would pity me and I wouldn't want them to stay with me because they felt sorry for me.

When the time came in mine and Martin's relationship where I would usually do something to push him away, something made me not want to do it. The time I had spent with him had changed me. I guess I was growing up...very slowly I might add, but it was happening. Martin treated me differently than anyone had ever treated me before. He respected me. He treated me like an adult. He encouraged me to pursue goals. He wanted me to be a better person. He expected me to be a better person. He expected me to be an adult and this was a little scary. Most of the time, I was proud and happy about being an adult, but a small part of me longed for the carefree days of before, when all I worried about was where the next party was. I didn't understand this because I didn't even like the person I used to be. So why was I missing her?

I decided that instead of sabotaging our relationship, I would tell him about what happened to me. It seemed like the next logical step. But how was I going to tell him?

"I thought you should know that when I was seventeen I was abducted by a stranger, raped, almost killed and because of that I'm kind of a shattered freak who will never be normal. Hope that's ok.

Hey, do you want to catch a movie later?"

That's not exactly how it went but it felt just as awkward. I also told him about my alter ego...party girl...and how I was really just an empty, pitiful shell.

He said that he always knew that's not who I really was. He loved me because he could see through that. He loved me for the way I treated people with kindness and fairness no matter who they were. He loved me for the way I always befriended the "underdog" who no one wanted to be friends with. He said he could see that I truly loved people and wanted to help them. He said I had a beautiful heart. He loved my dedication and my desire to do a good job. He loved my sense of humor AND my vulnerability. He told me that he knew from the first moment he met me, all those years ago, that I was the girl he was going to marry.

Oh, Martin! How is it possible that you exist?!?

"Therefore I will not keep silent; I will speak out in the anguish of my spirit, I will complain in the bitterness of my soul."

Job 7: 11

To the Members of the Parole Board-1995

In December of 1994, I received a letter from the District Attorney's office. It read...

Dear Jurney,

Please be advised that the above-named defendant is scheduled to appear before the Board of Parole in February 2001. As the victim in this case, you may want to make your concerns known to the Parole Board. To do so, you can write a letter to the following address:

Blah
Blah
Blah, NY

So I wrote a letter. Actually, I wrote two letters, but I could only find one of them. Sorry.

To the members of the Parole Board, 1995,

My name is Jurney. I am the victim in this particular case. Mr. Smith received a sentence of 15-25 years in prison for rape. I wrote earlier to voice my opinion about Mr. Smith's parole hearing in February 2001. Something else came to my attention that I would like to share with you.

In my previous letter I mentioned that "rape is a hate crime. People who rape do not learn NOT to offend again. They are sick. They will rape again." I have sent you a newspaper clipping in the hope that I may use it as an example.

In the clipping it states how in 1972 Stephen Waite robbed a convenience store. In the process he "dragged a 14 year old girl from the store and pushed her into a stolen car, where he taped her mouth and hands." Then he raped her and forced her to engage in sodomy. Mr. Waite received a life sentence for the robbery/rape, but he only served 16 years. SIXTEEN YEARS! "Waite was released on lifetime parole in 1989."

Then, on November 17, 1994, Waite abducted a 36 year old man from his van on Interstate 81. "Waite handcuffed the man cut him with a knife and repeatedly sodomized him."

What happened to the 14 year old girl in 1972 was very tragic. What happened to the 36 year old man in 1994 could have been avoided if Mr. Waite had served his life sentence.

I don't know if you have ever been brutally offended in a way such as rape, but I have. Even though the actual offense may not take much time, the emotional pain lasts a lifetime.

You might say I received a life sentence with no hope for parole. Maybe it would help if you explained to me why people who commit such brutal crimes even qualify for parole. Maybe then I'll understand a little better.

So while I'm serving my life sentence, Mr. Smith, convicted rapist and attempted murderer, gets a parole hearing after serving only 10 years. When do I get my so called parole hearing?

Sincerely,
Jurney Eve

To which they responded...

Dear Ms Eve:

I am responding to your recent correspondence in which you are discussing the parole of Mr. Smith.

For your information, Mr. Smith is serving a minimum term of 10 years and a maximum term of 20 years and will make his initial Parole Board interview in February 2001.

"(Oh, thanks for setting me straight. I thought his sentence was 15-25 years. My mistake.)"

I would like to offer you an opportunity to make your statement in person to a member of the Parole Board.

"(At that time the Parole Board member would take your statement and put them in memorandum form and those statements would be put in a confidential file for the Parole Board panel to review.)"

In return, the member of the Parole Board would discuss the circumstances of the sentence, factors that the Parole Board considers in determining release and answer any of your questions.

You should be aware, however, that the Parole Board member who interviews you, may not be the Parole Board member that will be sitting on the Parole Board panel before Mr. Smith and that this meeting would be conducted only one time.

Sincerely,
Mr. Dumbass

I did not like this letter. It felt like they were mocking me with their air of superiority. Their insensitive and formal response upset me. They would interview me? Was I applying for a job? It was hard enough to write the letter in the first place. I wasn't about to go down there and tell my story to a stranger...again. A stranger that "may not be the Parole Board member that will be sitting on the Parole Board panel before Mr. Smith" the day of his Parole hearing.

No thank you!

"Therefore do not worry about tomorrow, for tomorrow will worry about itself."

Matthew 6: 34

Mary Lou

The day I found out I was pregnant...well; I'm not going to lie. I was terrified! I was happy, but I was worried, too. How could I take care of a baby when I couldn't even take care of myself? What if I screwed this child up? I was so afraid of being responsible for the care and welfare of another human being. My best friend Leigh remembers me calling her crying because I was so afraid of this new responsibility.

Don't get me wrong. I fell in love with this child the moment I found out I was pregnant. Loving the baby was never the problem, protecting the baby was. How could I bring a baby into this world? This horrible, God abandoned world. The more I thought about this the more heart-broken I was. The fact was I couldn't protect this child from everything no matter how hard I tried.

For the next nine months, I alternated between ecstatic and terrified. Martin, on the other hand, remained calm. He did not share my irrational fear of the unknown. I also discovered that it is much harder to name your child than the world lets onto? This child would be stuck with this name for the rest of their life. I had to make sure it didn't rhyme with anything unflattering. Imagine the name calling!

I knew I was having a girl, and I always knew that I wanted to name my first daughter after my mother's mother who died in 1981. I didn't get to spend a lot of time with her, but what little time we did spend together really left an impression on me. The only problem I was faced with was that she had an incredibly old-fashioned name. I tried quirky twists on it and I thought I had one picked out until I went to visit my grandfather one day.

He said to me, "I'm so glad you're naming your daughter after your grandmother. Nothing makes me happier. I know she'd be proud." So, there it was. It had been decided. My daughter would have an old-fashioned family name. I named her Mary Lou.

"Your beginnings will seem humble, so prosperous will your future be."

Job 8: 7

Motherhood

I found out that being a good mother is NOT a gift bestowed upon you at the birth of your first child. There are no books that can fully prepare you for it. I had never babysat before so I knew nothing except what I had read in the popular book, "What to expect when you're expecting", which is a great book, by the way. I highly recommend it. But the books can only take you so far.

Luckily, one of my new friends knew a great deal about babies. She babysat all the time. She loved babies. It came so naturally to her. It was, as if it were her calling. Her name was Mae and we had become really good friends. I loved her. She could make me laugh when I didn't feel like laughing. She was one of those people that you wanted to be around because her good mood was infectious.

Mae said she would help me out with Mary Lou. She moved in with Martin and me for a few months and taught me everything she knew about babies. She was amazing. If it wasn't for her, I would've never slept. Mae was such a prominent figure in my daughter's life that she became known as "Nanny".

It took me about three months to get the hang of everything and even then I was no expert. Our daughter taught me something new every day. For example, when feeding cereal through a bottle feeder you should make sure the hole in the nipple isn't too big...Ouch...do not leave the baby alone with a kitten...Ouch...and another big one, if you put her down she WILL cry.

I had a lot of help. Between Martin, Mae, Martin's mother and my mother, we always had a babysitter. Our daughter was loved by many, and I would make it my mission to make sure she knew just how loved she was. I vowed to never let one day pass where I didn't tell her how much I loved her. The thing was I wasn't the only one to make a vow to Mary Lou. Reverend Jane had vowed to teach her only grandchild about God.

I saw no harm in this. After all, it was a guaranteed and trustworthy babysitter, every Sunday morning.

"Therefore the law is paralyzed, and justice never prevails. The wicked hem in the righteous, so that justice is perverted."

Habakkuh 1: 4

Injustice

Shortly after the birth of my daughter, I received another letter from the District Attorney's office. Apparently, Mr. Smith had been keeping himself busy behind bars. The District Attorney sent me a copy of a letter that she had sent to the Parole Board on my behalf. It read...

Dear Sir or Madam:

Enclosed please find copies of two letters recently sent by the above-named defendant to the librarian of the *Small Town USA Library seeking yearbook photographs of his "step-sister", Jurney. I am deeply concerned about these letters because Jurney is not the defendant's step-sister; she is the victim of rape for which he is currently serving his state prison term.

I am sure you are familiar with the facts underlying the defendant's conviction. On the afternoon of April 28, 1991, the defendant was driving his truck on *Route 66 in *Small Town USA when he spotted Jurney, a seventeen year old high school student, riding her bicycle on the side of the road. The driver hit Jurney with his truck and then, under the guise of helping her, drove her to a secluded area. There he took Jurney from the truck, covered her head and tied her up, stripped her and raped her. Then, as he went back to his truck to obtain what Jurney thought was a shotgun, Jurney ran naked from the scene to a nearby residence.

There is no doubt in my mind that the defendant would have killed Jurney if she had not been brave enough and strong enough to outrun him.

You should also be aware that after the defendant was sentenced to state prison, he wrote to me on two occasions, requesting an opportunity to contact Jurney as a part of his "therapy" at the facility. I did contact Jurney to see if she was would be willing to hear from the defendant. When I received no response, I advised the defendant that it appeared Jurney was not willing to have any contact with him. Copies of that correspondence are also enclosed.

While I did not make any inquiries from the Parole Office at the time, I am now concerned, in light of the defendant's current request for photographs of Jurney, as to whether the defendant's desire to contact Jurney was part of any legitimate therapy program he was attending at the facility.

I have had an opportunity to speak recently with Jurney about the defendant's current attempts to obtain her photograph. She is understandably upset and frightened by the defendant's efforts and his continued interest in her. An order of protection had not been issued for Jurney at the time of the defendant's sentencing because there was no reason to believe that there would be any contact between the defendant and Jurney ever again. It was clearly a mistake on my part to believe that Jurney would be safe once the defendant went to prison.

I am hoping, however, that your office will be able to do something to stop the defendant's efforts to obtain information and/or photographs of Jurney or to make any attempts to contact her from prison.

In addition, I would ask that this information be considered by the Parole Board in deciding whether to ever release the defendant on parole. I believe that his effort to surreptitiously obtain Jurney's photograph demonstrates the danger he will pose to her and to other young women should he be released on parole.

Please let me know what, if anything can be done to stop the defendant from requesting information about Jurney while in prison. I will do everything I can to see that she is safe and free from danger and interference from the defendant.

Sincerely,
Ms. Tenderheart

I love that line..."I will do everything I can to see that she is safe and free from danger from the defendant." How beautiful is that line? This woman cares about me.

Years later, I was told that Mr. Smith threatened to kill her too. He somehow, from the confines of his maximum security prison cell, obtained her home address and her home phone number and sent a threatening letter to her. I was told they didn't know how he did this because her professional name is not her real name and her home address and phone number are listed under her real name. Not even HER real name but her husband's name.

How did he find her information? I think prisoners require more supervision. What do you think?

"But the day of the Lord will come like a thief."

2 Peter 3: 10

Still Angry

As Mary Lou grew, so did my love for her. How can someone love another person as much as I loved her? Sometimes I would just look at her and start crying because I couldn't believe that she existed and that she was mine. I may be a little biased, but my daughter was the smartest, cutest, most amazing child in the world. No really, she was!

She was also extremely blessed with an extended family of people that showered her with affection. I had kept my vow so far. She knew she was loved. Reverend Jane had also kept her vow. She took her to church every week and my daughter LOVED it. By age three, she could sing about Jesus; she could tell you about Jesus; and she could pray for your soul...which she did before every meal.

Sometimes she would ask me, "Mommy, why don't you go to church?" Or my personal favorite... "Are you and Daddy gonna get to go to Heaven?" I would answer, "Because I have to work." and "Of course, we will go to Heaven." All the things I felt you were supposed to say to a child, but I knew they weren't true. I could get Sundays off if I asked and I wasn't sure of anything when it came to Heaven.

After three years of watching my daughter attend church and seeing how much positive influence it had on her I still couldn't bring myself to go with her. After a few years, I began to believe in God again but I wasn't sure I wanted anything to do with Him. He had let me down and I was still angry.

In 1999, the church my daughter attended was hosting a production called "Heaven's Gate & Hell's Flames." Reverend Jane really wanted me to go. She said it was a really good production. So good, in fact, that it traveled from church to church all throughout the country because it had an amazing message. I was intrigued. How could a religious production be as good as she said it was? So I went.

"I seek You with all my heart; do not let me stray from Your commands."

Psalm 119: 10

Heaven's Gate & Hell's Flames

Heaven's Gate & Hell's Flames changed my life. The story was simple enough. It takes you into people's lives. You get a quick glimpse at how they live their life and whether or not they believed in Jesus. Then, you see their death and their descent into Hell or their rise into Heaven. You may think this sounds lame but it wasn't for me. It scared me senseless. I was fighting back tears as hard as I could, but they still came.

At the end of the production, the pastor asked if anyone wanted to ask Jesus into their hearts or if they wanted to recommit their life to Him and I did. I cannot explain to you the feeling of peace that I felt at that moment. I walked up to the alter in front of a few hundred people that were there and I knelt and prayed.

It was awkward and exhilarating at the same time. It's hard to believe that was only ten years ago. Through those ten years, I have been a faithful Christian and I have been a struggling Christian. I'm sorry to say, that those ten years weren't always spent praising Jesus, but I have always loved Him and believed in Him throughout those years.

Everyone stumbles from time to time. EVERONE! Nobody's perfect. A friend of mine once said, "When life knocks you on your knees that puts you in the perfect position to pray." That is so true. After all that I had been through, I began to realize that sometimes you HAVE to walk through the valley and experience what's in there for yourself in order to recognize and appreciate what you'll find when you come out. The path that leads us to God is different for everyone. You cannot take my path. You have to make your own.

That day in 1999 was the day that the giant hole in my heart began to heal. Slowly, very slowly.

"Train a child in the way he should go, and when he is old he will not turn from it."

Proverbs 22: 6

Sink or Swim

When I became a Christian in 1999, things around me slowly felt like they were falling into place. I started going to church on Sundays. I even started going to Bible study on Wednesday evenings. I found that I was happy a lot of the time for no particular reason. I stopped feeling sorry for myself and I started feeling hopeful that maybe someday I would be "normal." They say that Jesus heals all pain and that all you have to do is ask for Him to heal you. So I was hopeful.

I knew I wouldn't be healed overnight but I figured maybe one day I would forget all about what happened to me. Well, I'm sure I wouldn't forget entirely, but surely, it would become a faded memory that didn't cause me so much pain. Eventually, I would be able to associate sex with love and I would stop looking at EVERY male as a potential rapist.

One evening, during Bible study, the pastor mentioned the church's need for workers in the children's ministries, specifically the Wednesday evening youth group, and it was like a bell went off in my head. I wanted to work with children. I wanted to be a positive influence in a little girl's life the way the leaders in my youth group were to me when I was a little girl. I believe that because of the time I spent in church when I was a child, even if it was such a short time, had a tremendous impact on the direction my life was taking now. I gave my heart to the Lord when I was nine years old and even though I turned my back on God as I grew, He never turned His back on me. I believe that He was always with me but I chose to turn a blind eye to Him.

So, I became a worker in the kindergarten girls' class, and boy did I work. When the pastor mentioned they needed help he wasn't kidding. I was given a giant book full of everything I would need to know and pointed toward my classroom full of twelve rambunctious, beautiful, talkative five year olds. Talk about sink or swim!

There were times when I wanted to pull my hair out and scream while running from the room, but I'll tell you, the year I spent with those little girls was one of the best times of my life. I learned so much from them. Being placed in that situation forced me to get into the word of God. I had twelve little girls who looked to me for spiritual guidance and answers to their questions that sometimes I didn't know the answers to, but we found the answers together. Being a mentor to someone, especially a child, gave me such joy. I found that as I encouraged them to seek the Lord, I also encouraged myself. As I taught them, they taught me.

I volunteered every Wednesday until September 2000 when I had to take a couple of months off to give birth to my beautiful baby boy who we named Martin Jr. Another good thing that happened to me during that year was I finally became Mrs. Martin.

"Do not judge, or you too will be judged."

Matthew 7: 1

My New Job

Martin and I agreed after Mary Lou was born that as long as we could afford it, one of us would be a stay-at-home parent. We agreed that we wouldn't pay someone else to help raise our kids if we didn't have to. Martin made more money than me and I was more than happy volunteering to be the one who stayed home. I fell into that lifestyle easily. I enjoyed being domesticated. Who would've thought?

Since 1996, I did have a few part-time jobs, but nothing that would interfere with our children's lives. This was our arrangement until 2001 when I became restless. As much as I enjoyed being a stay-at-home mom, a part of me felt guilty. I felt like I wasn't contributing enough. Of course, I knew this wasn't true. I was contributing just as much as Martin. Just because it wasn't a monetary contribution didn't make it any less significant, but nevertheless, I became restless. Martin, who was also feeling restless at his job, agreed to a role reversal.

In November of 2001, I took a job at the only thing I was qualified to do. I got a job as a restaurant manager and Martin slid into the role of Mr. Mom. I was very excited about this new venture. This would be my first salaried job. I was actually surprised that I even got the job. I did have experience as a restaurant supervisor but there's quite a difference between supervising a fast food chain and managing a full service restaurant. I was later told by my fellow managers that some of the other job candidates were more qualified than me but I got the job because I was "cuter." True story.

I remember before I went away for training, as you usually do when you take a job for a restaurant management position, Reverend Jane sat me down and explained to me the importance of spending time with Jesus everyday by praying and reading my Bible. She said it was important to surround myself with other Christians and if I spent too much time with people who weren't Christians, I would find it hard to remain faithful. She said, "You're only as good as the company you keep."

But I wasn't worried. I considered myself a strong, Christian woman whose faith would not be tested. After all, didn't Jesus spend a lot of His time with sinners? "He must needs go whom the devil driveth," right? Besides, who knows, my new co-workers could be completely wonderful people. Who are we to judge?

"For though a righteous man falls seven times, he rises again."

Proverbs 24: 16

Stressed Out!

I took that job with the best of intentions. I was going to be the best I could be. I was going to be the best manager there. I worked very hard to prove that I deserved that job. Not to toot my own horn, but I had/have a fantastic work ethic which makes it easy for me to succeed. My problem is I also have an easily influenced mind which means I quickly pick up on the emotions and attitudes of those around me.

While my co-workers weren't bad people, and some were even Christians, I found myself gravitate toward the ones who seemed really misguided. I think it's because the misguided ones are usually the ones who are misunderstood, and therefore, somewhat shunned by others, and I can't stand seeing people left out. I befriend them, thinking I will be a positive influence to them, but it usually doesn't work that way. It wasn't long before Martin found me coming home at three am because I decided to go have a few drinks with my "new friends".

In the year and a half that I had that job, I completely stopped going to church. I didn't have time. I worked sixty hours a week. My two year old son didn't seem to know who I was. He wouldn't come to me and it broke my heart. I was under so much stress. I was losing track of what was best for me. I was practically anorexic. I was 5'5" and I only weighed 102 lbs. Size zero was too big for me. Of course, it also could've been because of the letter I received in the spring of 2002. It read...

Dear Jurney,

I am writing to advise you that when Mr. Smith met with the Parole Board, release was denied. There is, however, a provision in the corrections law that allows inmates to earn good time and reduce the amount of time served in confinement. This is known as a conditional release.

Whether an inmate is released by action of the Parole Board or by conditional release, he or she is supervised by the Division of Parole until the sentence is discharged or the completion of the imposed period of Post Release Supervision.

If all allowable good time is earned, Mr. Smith is scheduled to be conditionally released on November 28, 2005.

If you have any questions or need additional information, please feel free to contact this unit at the above address or at (123) 456-7890.

Sincerely,
Some Random Parole Officer

Yeah, I had questions! What is a conditional release? Will it be granted to him or is this just a standard letter sent out to everyone? He hasn't earned all allowable good time so, surely, I have nothing to worry about...right?

"Pray continually."

1 Thessalonians 5: 17

Conditional Release

After a little research, I have come to the conclusion that a prisoner's conditional release means they have served 7/10 of their sentence and as long as they haven't committed a "punishable" offense while in prison, they are released...regardless of whether or not the Parole Board has granted them parole. You follow?

I, obviously, have nothing to worry about. My attacker has committed a "punishable" offense while in prison. He's threatened lives and tried to contact his victim. Those MUST be "punishable" offenses, right? WRONG! Apparently, they are not because he was STILL scheduled to be released on November 28, 2005. To the utmost dismay of the NY State police, the Parole Board, the judge whose life and family he threatened to kill, the D.A. whose life he threatened, his ex-wife whose life he threatened, and a few prison guards, not to mention myself, he was still going to be released after serving fourteen years.

The judicial system...OUR judicial system, the one that's supposed to protect us from people like him, was indeed setting him free. As a parting gift, they probably would have handed him a smut magazine and a revolver. Isn't that something? Everyone involved in this case KNOWS he shouldn't be released. They KNOW he's still dangerous and that he's NOT rehabilitated but, because of the underlining laws, there's not much they can do about it.

However, first he must find a suitable place to live before they'll turn him loose on society. He's been trying to find one since 2005 and so far he's been unsuccessful. I guess there is something they can do after all.

His parents don't even want him. There are only so many places in NYS that are not near a school or a playground. There are certain criteria that must be met before the Parole Board will approve an address for him. I'm not sure what they are, but I do know that eventually he will find one. They can't keep him forever and it WILL be somewhere in upstate NY.

So, not that it will do much to protect you, but I hope all you "Upstaters" live near a school or a playground or you might just discover that your new neighbor isn't so "neighborly."

"But now trouble comes to you, and you are discouraged; it strikes you, and you are dismayed. Should not your piety be your confidence and your blameless ways your hope?"

Job 4: 5-6

To the members of the Parole Board 2002

To respond to the most recent letter about Mr. Smith's conditional release and any future parole hearings, I decided to write a letter of my own. It read...

To the members of the Parole Board,

How do I begin to explain to you how Mr. Smith has affected my life? When I was seventeen years old, he kidnapped me, raped me repeatedly and tried to kill me. I am almost twenty-nine years old now and I think of that man every day. I think of all the things he did to me. How they affect my everyday life. Such as, I can no longer ride a bicycle. This may sound trivial to you but I used to ride ten miles, sometimes every day. I loved it! I have not gotten on a bike since the day he hit me off of mine with his truck, cutting my head open with his passenger's side mirror.

I no longer trust anyone because of the way he mislead me to believe that if I got into his truck he would take me to the hospital. Instead, he threatened me with a large ice pick. I do not feel secure in the confines of my own home. I am constantly looking for possible hiding places. My doors and windows are always locked. If I hear a noise I search the entire house for possible intruders. In public it's worse. I'm constantly looking over my shoulder. I think the worst of everyone I see.

My relationships suffer as well. Everyone I have ever had, other than my current one, has ended because of my inability to associate sex with love. Sex is not a beautiful thing that two people share. When two people are in love there is no need for sex. Try explaining that to your significant other. I am married now. My husband and I have had this argument. I try to tell him that "it's not you, it's me" but he doesn't understand. How could he? Why would I not want to have sex with the man I love? He asks me if I really love him. He wonders if I even find him attractive. So, I make myself have sex with him once a week because I don't want him to feel inadequate. It's not his fault I feel this way. It's Mr. Smith's.

So I live in this bubble where everyone thinks I'm a remarkably strong person for dealing with this so well, but it's a lie. I am petrified of Mr. Smith. I'm terrified that he will find me and my family. I have children now and I am concerned for their safety. Mr. Smith tried to obtain pictures of me in 1996. He wrote a few letters to my hometown library, telling them he was my step-brother and that he wanted my senior picture. Why would he want pictures of me? I believe it was so he can remember what I look like so when he gets paroled he can come find me. Why else would he want pictures of me?

I read in the paper the other day about a man who was arrested with drugs on him. He could receive up to twenty five years in prison. Mr. Smith will only serve fourteen years before he is released on November 28, 2005. Fourteen years! He has messed up my head for the rest of my life but will only serve fourteen years?!? I don't want to sound like a selfish person. I believe in second chances. If I thought that he wasn't going to try to find me, I would let him go without a fight. I believe he blames me for his incarceration and he WILL find me.

Someone within the system told me that statistics show that sex offenders have a high risk of repeat offense. If he doesn't harm me he will harm someone else. Maybe someone can explain to me why a person who rapes another person of their trust, their security, their ability to love and their innocence would only serve fourteen years when statistics show that they will harm someone else. Maybe this time he'll kill! Sex offenders are incurable!

To sum this all up, I do not think that Mr. Smith should be released on parole and I do not think he should be released on November 28, 2005 either. I do think it is ridiculous that he will only serve fourteen years total when sex offenders are incurable. When he is released, I want to exercise my full rights as the victim. I want to know where he will live. What the phone number of his Parole Officer is. I do not want him within 200 miles of whatever county, of whichever state I happen to be living in at that particular time. I do not want him to contact me in any way.

I get a feeling of hopelessness when I think about my rights as the victim. If he finds me, what really can the law do to stop him? The law didn't stop him before. Why would it stop him when he is free? When am I free? Where is my justice?

The Victim,
Jurney

"If a blind man leads a blind man, both will fall into the pit."

Matthew 15: 14

Lessons Learned

After one and a half years of working at my new job, I began to suspect that the reason I was so miserable was because I had completely cut God out of my life...again. I no longer felt his presence, even when I prayed. My "new friends" were not positive influences and I wasn't the positive influence to them that I originally thought I would be. Reverend Jane was right. You're only as good as the company you keep.

I began to pray for the Lord to come into my life again. I asked Him to show me what He wanted me to do. I said to Him, "Lord, only You know what's best for my life. You know I am unhappy because of the path my life seems to be taking. I put my troubles into Your hands. Do with me what only You know needs to be done. I surrender everything to You, Lord."

I must have prayed that prayer for a month before something happened, and let me tell you, something definitely happened. I learned that when you ask for the Lord's help you better be ready because when He decides to help you, things usually get worse before they get better.

What happened to me taught me more than one thing. It taught me to always follow rules; I was not cut out to be a successful restaurant manager; do not make friends with your employees; be prepared for the worst; and to trust God. I ended up losing my job because of my own insecurities. Lessons learned.

"For your enemies will be clothed in shame, and the tents of the wicked will be no more."

Job 8: 22

Lucky

I almost had a nervous breakdown in 2003. We no longer had an income coming in because of me. How were we going to pay our bills? What were we going to do? I was a basket case but Martin was a rock. He's very good with money, and fortunately, he believed in saving for a rainy day. And this was definitely our rainy day. We had enough money to live on and keep our bills paid for three months so he assured me that I had nothing to worry about. We decided that Martin would go back to work and I would stay home again.

Within two months, Martin had a job that paid better than any either of us had had before. Things seemed to be falling into place but I couldn't shake the new feelings that were welling up inside of me because of the conditional release letter. I always knew that one day Mr. Smith would get out of prison, but I tried not to think about it too much. Now, my biggest fear was becoming a reality.

For the past twelve years, I had been barely dealing with the consequences of what he'd already done to me. I wasn't ready to deal with all the new ways he could hurt me once he was free. Every time I received another letter about Mr. Smith, I was reminded that there is a man in this world who wanted to hurt me.

My greatest fear wasn't that he would hurt ME. My greatest fear was, and still is, that he will hurt my children. How can I protect them? When do I explain this to them? When he is released, should I warn my friends??? My church leaders??? My children's schools??? He's a very cunning man. It seems to me that he might try to go through someone I know to find me. I wouldn't want to be responsible if he hurt someone I loved if I could've stopped it simply by telling them my story so that they would be aware.

Of course, it is possible that he won't try to find me. Maybe I'll get lucky and he'll leave me alone. But I always come back to...what if he doesn't???

"Do not be terrified; do not be discouraged, for the Lord your God will be with you wherever you go."

Joshua 1: 9

Precautions

As November 28, 2005 got closer, I thought about Mr. Smith's release more and more. It made me feel so helpless. I tried to think of every precaution I could take to make it difficult for him to find me should he choose to. We used a P.O. Box instead of our home address. I had no bank accounts or credit cards in my name. We had moved out of state. I didn't use the Internet because I was afraid I might leave some information that he could use to find me and I had a new last name.

I called my contact within the NY State police department and gave him my new address. He got in touch with my local authorities and explained my situation to them. He faxed me a recent picture of Mr. Smith and advised me to talk to my daughter's school. He said it would be a good idea to make them aware of the situation as well. I was already considering this so when he suggested it I knew it was the right thing to do.

Awkward...difficult...embarrassing...but never-the-less, I knew I needed to do it.

The next morning, I took the picture down to my daughter's school and told the principal the abridged version of my story. I made sure that they knew that I was the ONLY person authorized to pick my daughter up from school. Not even my husband...ONLY ME! I didn't want there to be any confusion. That was a really stressful year for me.

"Take no thought for the morrow: for the morrow shall take thought for the things of itself."

Matthew 6: 34

Secret Word

So, here it is, fall of 2005. It is only two months from Mr. Smith's conditional release date. I had taken whatever precautions I could think of to protect myself and my family from him. Other than the precautions that I mentioned before, I had told my close friends (all three of them) and my parents, but I still hadn't told my children.

By 2005, I had three children. My oldest was nine. My son was five and my newest addition was six months old, a little girl whom we named Sally. I decided that the only one of them who was on a need-to-know basis was my oldest. She went to school, where as my other two didn't and because of that they never left my side. But how do you tell a nine year old this story? I didn't want to scare her but I also wanted her to be safe.

I finally decided to have another "danger of strangers" conversation with her. I once again went over how you shouldn't talk to strangers. I gave her some examples of ways bad people might lure you away with them. Like, "Little girl, will you help me find my puppy because she's lost?" or, "Do you want some candy?" or, "Little girl, can you help me find my way?" I told her that there is safety in numbers and that she shouldn't go places alone. I said most bad people won't bother you if you are with friends. They look for the children who are by themselves. I told her anything I could think of to protect her, not only from "my monster", but all the monsters out there.

She asked me why would bad people want to take children and I didn't know how to answer her. I certainly couldn't say "for sex." She didn't even know what sex was yet and I wasn't ready to have that conversation.

One traumatic conversation at a time please.

I answered her as vaguely as I could. I said, "To do bad things to them. To hurt them." Then she asked me if I ever knew anyone who was taken by a bad person and my heart started pounding. I hadn't planned on telling her about my abduction but before I could stop myself (and sadly, that happens often) I said, "Yes...I was."

I ended up telling her about how I went for a bike ride all by myself and a bad man took me. She asked, "Did he do bad things to you?" I said, "Yes."

She asked, "Did it hurt?" I said, "Yes. That's why I never want that to happen to you."

When it looked like she was going to cry, I gave her a big hug. I told her not to cry because I was alright and I smiled at her. I told her how much I loved her and how much she meant to me. Inside, my heart was breaking. I had made my little girl cry. Maybe I shouldn't have told her about my abduction. But the damage had already been done.

Together, we decided to come up with a secret word that only we would know. The secret word could be used in an array of different situations, such as, if someone tells her that I sent them to pick her up and give her a ride home she could ask them what the secret word was. If they didn't know it then I didn't send them. Another way we thought of using the secret word was if she was in a situation that she didn't feel comfortable in, such as, at a friend's house, she could call me and say the secret word and I would know that she wanted to come home.

Although she loved the idea of having a secret word, she wasn't very good at using it. I would test her from time to time and she would always fail. I would send my friend to school to pick her up and she would NEVER ask my friend for the secret word. I would comfort myself by thinking that she didn't ask for the secret word because she knew this was my friend.

Over time, she's learned to use our secret word in different ways. Today, it's primarily used for those times when she has a friend over that is getting on her nerves and she wants her to go home. Hey, she's thirteen. At least she's being discreet.

"From the one who has been entrusted with much, much more will be asked."

Luke 12: 48

November 28, 2005

November 28, 2005 wasn't a very good day for me. After all, it was the day that the man who had kidnapped me, raped me, and tried to kill me was to be released from prison after only serving fourteen years of his measly twenty year sentence. Do I sound bitter? I'm sorry!

I had a really hard time thinking of anything else that day. I was assured by the authorities that I would receive a phone call the day he was released. NY State's way of keeping the victim informed. But by that evening, I had not received that phone call. I was anxious, irritable, scared, sad, angry, annoyed, worried...I was so many different emotions all at once that I didn't know what to do with myself. I spent most of the day sitting on my couch with a blank expression on my face. I didn't talk to anyone but I also didn't remind anyone why I was upset. They must have thought I was losing my mind.

The next morning, I called my connection at the NY State Police Department. He told me that Mr. Smith hadn't been released yet because he couldn't find a place to live that the Parole Board members considered suitable. He wanted to go back to the county where he had committed the crime but they didn't want him anywhere near there. It made sense. All of the people whose lives he had ruined, and since threatened, his ex-wife and child, the judge, the DA, a few prison guards...hearing that this man is coming back to your town, may feel like a death sentence.

However, the local and state police felt differently. They wanted him there. They wanted him close so they could keep a very close eye on him. Most of them remembered his crime all too well. Stuff like that doesn't happen too often in upstate NY. They felt that another county's police department might not have the same emotional attachment to this case as they all had.

In the end, it was up to the Parole Board and they denied his address request. He put in another address request. This time he asked to go live with his parents in a different area of upstate, but his parents denied that request. They didn't want him.

He started contacting churches, asking the pastors for help in finding a place to live. Some actually tried to help him. After all, they're so trusting and caring. They believe in second chances and doesn't everyone deserve forgiveness. I told you he was cunning. Some found him shelters that specialized in helping recently released inmates get back on their feet. Oh yeah! They exist! Is there one near you?

The Parole Board denied these address requests as well. I'm not sure why. Maybe they were near schools or playgrounds. I didn't really care WHY they denied him. I was just happy they had. What I wasn't happy about was the fact that I had told everyone about his release and why they should be watchful...for no reason. I wasn't mad. I know they didn't know the Parole Board was going to deny his address request. I knew what I did was necessary. Although, I should have waited until he was actually released before I told everyone. I thought about waiting until then but I thought they would appreciate a little head's up in case they needed to take a few precautions of their own. Oh well. It was good practice...I guess.

"The Lord is good to those whose hope is in Him, to the one who seeks Him."

Lamentations 3:25

Summer 2006

By the summer of 2006, Mr. Smith had still not been released from prison. The Parole Board was denying every address request he made. The NY State Police told me that this could continue until 2011, when his sentence was up, but they wanted me to be prepared because they could approve an address request and release him as well.

That summer was a big one for my family because we moved...again. A different state, a different police department, a different school system.

When the school year started, I contacted the principal and the local and state police departments. I gave them the picture of Mr. Smith and explained my situation to them. I knew there was a chance that he wouldn't be released soon, but I decided it was better to be safe than sorry. This time around, it wasn't as hard. It was becoming easier to tell complete, strangers what had happened to me. Of course, they weren't getting the long and detailed version. Baby steps!

In all the chaos of being worried about Mr. Smith's impending release, I had let my relationship with God slip drastically. I hadn't been going to church regularly and I was so...sad...all...of...the...time! I didn't understand why it was still so painful to me. I stopped blaming God a long time ago. I knew that only through God would I learn to accept what had happened to me and heal. What I didn't expect was for it to still be so painful after all these years. I knew I wouldn't be healed overnight but I honestly thought I was getting there.

For years, I prayed for healing and I felt like it was slowly happening. It entered my thoughts less frequently. It seemed to hurt less and less as the years went by, but when I was faced with his impending release, all of the old emotions came flooding back and I felt as if all my progress wasn't progress at all. I still knew that only God could heal me. I guess I was just disappointed that it wasn't happening faster. Maybe I was praying for the wrong thing.

"Let us throw off everything that hinders and the sin that so easily entangles, and let us run with perseverance the race marked out for us."

Hebrews 12: 1

January 2007

By January of 2007, sixteen years had passed since April 28, 1991 and throughout those sixteen years, not a single day had gone by that I did not think about what had happened to me. I thought about how it had changed me and molded me. I felt like it controlled me and I hated that! I knew that by dwelling on it I gave it power. I gave him power, but I couldn't help it.

I was constantly reminded of that day by so many things. If I saw someone riding a bike; if I saw a man with a "beer belly"; if I saw a pickup truck; if I saw a policeman; every time I saw a woman jogging by herself. It took the simplest of everyday normality's to trigger my memory. I mean, it wasn't as if I broke down in tears every time I thought about it. It wasn't that painful anymore. When I thought about it, it mostly just made me sad because I couldn't let it go. I didn't know how to.

It's always worse for me around April. Every April, I try to think of something I can do for myself to help me heal. One year, I thought about writing Mr. Smith a letter, but I couldn't figure out what I wanted to say to him, so I never did. For a few years, I thought about seeing a counselor, but unless they could hypnotize me and make me forget, what were they going to do for me? Besides, did I really want to forget? As tragic as it was to be run down by a truck, kidnapped and raped, I would NOT be the same person I am today if it had never happened to me. I'm not saying I'm grateful, but I am stronger.

Usually on April 28th, I just mope around and wallow in my own self-pity. It's rather pathetic, I know. In April of 2007, I had two things in mind that I hoped would help me heal. First, I was going to buy myself a bicycle. I hadn't ridden one since that day and I thought just getting on one would be a huge step. I could buy Sally one of those child seats that you pull behind your bike so she could ride with me while my older two were in school. I wouldn't be alone. I'd have my daughter with me. Safety in numbers!

But then I started thinking about how vulnerable I would still be. How I would put my daughter at risk. Unless I could find another adult to ride with I would never feel safe. So I never bought one.

The second thing I was going to do that April was to write down my story. I had recently read a book called, "Lucky" by Alice Sebold. It's a true story about how Alice was raped while she was in college. I read that book with my mouth hanging open in shock. I couldn't understand how she could share such intimate details of such a traumatic experience with so many people. I admired her courage and it inspired me. So I got myself a shiny, new journal and I started writing about April 28, 1991.

Over the next three months, I got about half of my story out before I decided that it was too hard and I stopped. It was so emotionally draining. Trying to remember every detail that I had tried so hard to forget was making me really sad all of the time. It sat unfinished on a bookshelf where I would look at it from day to day with a disappointed feeling inside of me. I knew I needed to finish my story.

During that time, I started getting a strange feeling that I was somehow supposed to write this story. It came to me more and more as the months passed by. I couldn't shake it. I wasn't sure why but I thought, maybe it's because I had been praying for healing for so long and this was God's way of answering my prayer. He knew that by writing it down it would help me heal. I don't know and it's hard to explain but I felt like God wanted me to write my story. I started to think that maybe what I went through had a purpose.

But, there it sat, unfinished on my bookshelf until a friend of mine gave me an idea. Why not write it down on the internet? I could create a blog. I figured, if I put it on the internet for the whole world to see, I might feel obligated to finish it. So, I got a MySpace page.

I know, I know. Who uses MySpace anymore, but remember this was 2007 when MySpace was still cool.

The problem with that was I was afraid of the internet. As far as I was concerned, the internet was just another way for Mr. Smith to get information about me. I didn't want to leave a trail that would make it easier for him to find me.

Just another way I was letting him control me.

In the end, I put aside my fears and I decided to stop letting him control me and with the help of my tech-savvy husband, I created an account that would make it hard for someone to find me. Not impossible, but not easy either.

"Praise be to the God and Father of our Lord Jesus Christ, the Father of compassion and the God of all comfort, who comforts us in all our troubles, so that we can comfort those in any trouble with the comfort we ourselves have received from God."

2 Corinthians 1: 3-4

My First Blog

On April 18, 2007, I started telling my story on my new MySpace page. I had an incredibly small audience. I think I only had twelve readers but I didn't care. I had readers!

I didn't go into too much detail. I just talked about the actual crime. It was a very short blog, as far as blogs go. I think there were only thirteen entries in all. I can't actually count them because I deleted them soon after I had finished my story. But what a feeling!

I had just told anyone who happened to stumble upon my humble blog about the most intimately traumatic experience of my life! I was proud of myself for finally telling my story but the best thing about sharing my story with others was the responses I received from my readers. One of them wrote to me and said...

"I just wanted to tell you what an influence you have been to me over the last few days. I've been reading your blog and I realize that maybe sharing my story would help rid myself of some of the fears and anger that have been festering inside me for the last eleven years or so.

Thank you for letting me read your blog and know that someone else out there has felt the way I felt and lived.

Thank you for giving me the courage to let this weight go."

THAT FELT AMAZING!!! I still get teary-eyed every time I read that. I touched her life! I had helped someone just by sharing my story! I was so grateful that something good had come out of the most horrible thing that had ever happened to me and I wanted to help more people, but I didn't know how?

Not long after I received her message, another woman sent me a message, then another, and another. Hearing those women's stories had humbled me. It made me realize that I wasn't alone. Hearing their stories helped me the same way that hearing my story must have helped them. Most of them were looking for comfort, advice, support, friendship. Two of my closest friends to this day are my friends because of my blog. I couldn't believe all of the good that was happening simply because I chose to tell my story.

Over the course of writing my story, I've had women write to me and share their own stories. I instantly loved each and every one of them, not just for trusting me enough to tell me their stories, because some of them had never told another soul about their experience, but because I felt a certain camaraderie with them. We were helping each other. We are survivors!

I used to think that nobody could relate to what I went through. I naively assumed that no one had lived through as much as I had. I assumed that my pain was somehow worse than my friends' pain, but I was wrong. Hearing those women's stories has humbled me. My story pales in comparison to some of the stories I've heard. It was like a slap in the face. I actually felt stupid for believing for so long that my pain was somehow more significant than other people's pain. It was a very humbling experience for me.

Since 1991, all I heard was how I needed to go to a counselor. I needed to talk about what happened to me. That bottling up my emotions wasn't healthy and I was never going to feel better until I learned how to deal with it. But I never bought any of that. I didn't understand how talking about what happened to me could possibly make me feel any better. I didn't understand why bringing all that pain to the surface would do anyone any good.

It wasn't until sixteen years after I was raped that I finally learned that all of that is in fact true.

Imagine that!

"From the fruit of their lips people are filled with good things, and the work of their hands brings them reward."

Proverbs 12:14

Dream On

For a few months after my first blog, I dreamed about ways to help more people. I knew it was something I wanted to pursue but I couldn't figure out how. How could I get more people to read my story?

It was Alice Sebold who inspired me once again. I figured if she could find someone to publish her story then maybe I could find someone to publish mine. Of course Ms. Sebold is a brilliant writer and it doesn't hurt that she has a college degree, but I wasn't going to let that stop me. I went right to work. For the next year I turned my focus toward my new goal and when I had it to where I felt it was finished, I started sending my manuscript to every publisher I could find…at least I tried to send them. None of them would even humor me. They said "they weren't accepting manuscripts from authors that didn't have agents."

That was a minor setback. But I regrouped and turned my focus toward finding an agent. But wouldn't you know it? Agents weren't willing to represent unpublished authors. How was I going to get an agent if I wasn't a published author and how was I going to become a published author if I couldn't get an agent? It was very frustrating. In the end, I decided to research the less glamorous world of self publishing and as a result, on March 30, 2010, my book, Intended Harm, was released for the first time. And while I may have self published, it didn't change the fact that I was now a published author.

"We are hard pressed on every side, but not crushed; perplexed, but not in despair; persecuted, but not abandoned; struck down, but not destroyed."

2 Corinthians 4:8-9

A Disgruntled State of Shock

In the spring of 2010, I found myself in a disgruntled state of shock! Apparently NY has this new law called The Civil Confinement Law which enables the state to hold sex offenders longer than their sentence if they are deemed to have a mental illness that causes a lack of control over their behavior, and they are a danger to themselves or to society. There are only a handful of sex offenders that the state considers dangerous enough to attempt to have committed and Mr. Smith happens to be one of the lucky few. As a matter of fact, he happens to be one of the first. Of course, some people think this is a violation of the prisoner's constitutional rights; therefore, it is a little controversial. I would think this trial is going to be a pretty big deal in my small corner of NY.

They don't know if the papers will release my name. They don't know if I will have to testify. They don't know much of anything because they've never seen a trial like this before. But they do know it will most likely make the papers and the news. I have been told that I should prepare myself for the chance of it reaching the national news media as well.

A psychiatrist has already evaluated him and has deemed him to have a mental illness that causes him to be a sexual predator. He has been moved to a mental health facility so he can start his treatment for his mental illness while he waits for a trial date to be set. They are not sure when his trial will start. All they know is that it will happen sometime before April 28, 2011.

That trial will be where the final decision is made by the NY Supreme Court about whether or not he does indeed have a mental illness. If they agree that he does have a mental illness that causes him to be a sexual offender then one of two things could happen. They could decide that, although he has a mental illness, he is safe to live in the public as long as he is supervised by parole. He might even be made to wear a GPS ankle bracelet so his movements can be monitored. Or they could decide that he is too dangerous to live amongst the public and be sent back to the mental health facility for further treatment.

These are the only two options that are ok with me. The third option is, the Judge/Jury doesn't agree with the earlier psychiatrist and they think he does NOT have a mental illness, which is totally probable. I was told that he has always received a "clean bill of health" for mental illness while in prison so why would they change it now? If they disagree with the earlier psychiatrist and declare he does NOT have a mental illness then he walks free on April 28, 2011.

Well, almost. Thanks to Megan's Law, he will still have to register as a violent sex offender. Megan's Law is named after seven-year-old Megan Kanka, a New Jersey girl who was raped and killed by a known child molester who had moved across the street from the family without their knowledge. In the wake of the tragedy, the Kankas sought to have local communities warned about sex offenders in the area. All states now have a form of Megan's Law.

Under Megan's Law a predator like him would have to register as a level three sex offender. Level three offenders are the most violent and dangerous. When a level three or a level two offender is released from prison the community is notified. But because Megan's Law was put into effect after Mr. Smith was convicted he does not have to follow these guidelines. He will come out of prison as a level one sex offender. The community will not be notified. If you want information about a level one offender, you have to go down to your local police station and request it. As required by law, the DCJS, Division of Criminal Justice System, can only provide information on level two and level three offenders on their website.

He could move in right next to you and you would never know it. He could move in right next door to me and I would never know it. Even if I did know it, I could do nothing about it.

I felt violated all over again!

"So we fix our eyes not on what is seen, but on what is unseen, since what is seen is temporary, but what is unseen is eternal."

2 Corinthians 4:18

Civil Confinement Trial

Today is the day that Mr. Smith's civil commitment trial is scheduled to begin. This trial makes me very anxious. The emotional side of me wants him to be found mentally ill so that he won't be released and my life can continue on as usual. I mean, if he is released next year, I'm going to have to alter my entire life and my children's lives. They will no longer be able to walk to the bus stop without me, which is going to be a big alteration seeing how my daughter starts high school next year and her school starts two hours earlier than my other children's school does. I will have to wake my younger ones up earlier so we can all go to the bus stop with my oldest. There will be many other alterations but I'm choosing not to think about them too much. It isn't necessary yet.

Do you want to know something really weird? When I pray about this trial, I don't ask God for the jury to find him mentally ill so that he will be locked away longer. I just pray for God's Will to be done. I'm afraid that what God wants might be different than what I want and I know that what He wants is what's best for me. I know all too well that sometimes God's plans aren't the same as our plans. So, when I pray, I simply tell God that I trust Him and I know that no matter what the outcome of this trial is, it will be just another part of His amazing plan for my life.

"I have told you these things, so that in me you may have peace. In this world you will have trouble. But take heart! I have overcome the world."

John 16:33

The Sunday Paper

Yesterday, my whole family got up bright and early...well; we got up at 8am which IS bright and early for us on a weekend. We were going to drive to our hometown and visit my husband's family. We hadn't exchanged Christmas presents with them yet and my husband's baby sister had a baby of her own a month earlier and I had yet to cuddle and bond with him.

Once we were all packed for the night, loaded into the car, and getting ready to pull out of the driveway...one hour behind schedule...my phone rang. It was my friend Marie. I could tell she was upset about something because she sounded like she had been bawling. Her voice was shaky and she was out of breath. Once I got her to calm down, she told me there was an article in that morning's newspaper about Mr. Smith and it must have been a doosey because she was pretty upset over it. I was uncharacteristically calm about the news and I reassured her that it was ok. I told her I couldn't read it because I was driving but as soon as I got to my mother-in-laws' I would call her.

That was the longest 4 hour drive of my life. Actually, I spent 4 hours on the George Washington Bridge in NYC once. Now THAT was the longest 4 hour drive of my life. Four hours and I went four miles. I will never take the George Washington Bridge again!

So, four hours later, I arrived at my mother-in-laws and I finally got to read the article. I have changed the names to protect the innocent...and the ignorant.

WHAT PRICE IS TOO HIGH?

Mr. Smith spent 20 years in prison for raping a 17-year-old girl. Now a judge must decide whether to release him on parole or civilly commit him to a psychiatric facility at taxpayer cost of about $175K a year. After 20 years in prison, a man — who admitted he raped and would have killed his victim had she not escaped—could soon be released into the community. It will be up to a County Supreme Court Judge Ms. Frank to decide whether Mr. Smith, 48, should be released on parole, or be confined to a psychiatric facility under New York's civil commitment law. Smith has served his maximum sentence after pleading guilty in 1991 to first-degree rape, a felony.

According to court documents, he offered to help a 17-year-old girl after striking her with his pickup truck while she was riding her bike. But after she got into his truck, he tied her up, drove her to a secluded area and raped her. The girl got away, running into the woods when Smith returned to his truck to get his gun. He said he would have killed her to avoid being arrested.

Smith was in court on Thursday for a disposition hearing in his civil commitment case—the last step before a judge decides his fate. If confined, Smith would be committed to a psychiatric facility for treatment for at least one year. At the end of that year, he'd be up for a review and the court would determine if he had yet completed treatment and could go free, said Bruce Wayne, the assistant attorney general who is arguing on behalf of the state to civilly commit Smith. But under the civil commitment law, there is a requirement that four phases of treatment be completed, and no offenders are even near release more than three years after the program began in the state.

In 2007, state lawmakers approved civil commitment to route dangerous sex offenders whose sentences are ending into treatment in secure state psychiatric facilities. Now the state is coping with cost and space strains as a result of the program. The average annual price tag to treat sex offenders in secured facilities is about $175,000 per person, making New York's program the costliest of its kind in the nation.

SMITH'S CASE

Court documents show that before the 1991 incident, Smith had been convicted eight times for different crimes, with three of them involving a sexual element: A conviction for public lewdness; A burglary conviction which he plastered a woman's walls with clippings from pornographic magazines; And a felony count of first-degree unlawful imprisonment: Smith tried to kidnap two girls—one of whom was 10 years old—within hours of each other, Wayne said.

Following a petition from the attorney general's office to confine Smith to a psychiatric facility, a jury decided in November that Smith had a mental abnormality—a requirement to civilly commit a sex offender in New York. The only decision yet to be made in Smith's case is if he will be detained at such a facility, or if he will be released into the community on a parole-supervised program known as SIST, or Strict and Intensive Supervision and Treatment. Under SIST, offenders are required to wear GPS monitoring devices and are regularly subjected to polygraphs.

According to state data, eight of the 94 offenders ordered into SIST from 2007 through Nov. 30 are now charged with new sex crimes. Twenty-one others are accused of non-criminal, but sex related violations of their release terms.

THE TESTIMONY

In court Thursday, Frank—the County Supreme Court judge—heard conflicting testimony from two psychological experts on Smith's likelihood to reoffend. Clark Kent, a psychologist employed by the Office of Mental Health who testified on behalf of the state, warned that Smith was dangerous and needed to be detained. Kent said he had diagnosed Smith with antisocial personality disorder, sexual sadism and psychopathy.

"The triad puts him at the highest level we know of potential to reoffend," Kent said.

Lex Luthor, a Massachusetts-based psychologist who testified on behalf of the defense, disputed Kent's testimony. He argued Smith shouldn't have been diagnosed with such disorders, that testing methods used by Kent were unacceptable and that, even if he was a sexually sadistic psychopath, that doesn't necessarily predict a higher recidivism rate.

"Mr. Smith is a rapist," Luthor said. "I do not believe today he would be adequately diagnosed as a sexual sadist. Even if there is an element of sexual sadism, recent data shows very little to no correlation with the likelihood to reoffend."

Luthor also said because Smith has aged 20 years, his likelihood to commit another sex offense has decreased. An issue of concern, Kent said, was that Smith admitted during recent therapy sessions to having violent rape fantasies—something he said occurred before the 1991 incident. But Luthor insisted that Smith's admission was therapeutic, and a sign that he is trying to make progress.

Before adjourning and reserving her decision, the judge admitted this was an issue of concern.

"It's a troubling situation we find ourselves in now that, if you participate in therapy, you are kind of hanging yourself legally." Frank said. "But the defendant was in a court of law, not a counseling session", she added.

There's no clear timetable as to when Frank will issue a decision.

What this article fails to mention is that while Mr. Smith was serving twenty years in prison, he managed to obtain a few addresses of people involved in his case and send them threatening letters. He tracked me down a couple of times and he pretended to be my step-brother in the hopes someone would send him my picture. What this article also fails to mention is that because he was convicted before Megan's Law went into effect, he cannot be made to register as a level 3 sex offender.

But, honestly, I will be happy with whatever Judge Frank decides because whether he is confined to a mental health facility or strict parole, it's more than I ever expected. I've spent the last nineteen years thinking he's getting out and roaming free and there's nothing I can do about it. This is a victory for me.

Did this article make me angry? Yes! I felt that the reporter was saying that saving money was more important than our safety. And I just think that Lex Luthor is an idiot. But I've had a long time to prepare myself for things like this. Plus, I just have to marvel at God's timing because I can't help but think that if I never opened up and told my story, then this article would have devastated me. There is no doubt about it. I can only imagine what kind of hot mess I would be in at this very moment. But I DID publish my story for the whole world to read and because of that it no longer hurts to hear about.

What should have been a day of tears and binging for me, based on the past eighteen years was instead a day where I felt surrounded by love and support from my friends and family. The amount of support I have received reassures me that sharing my story was the right thing to do.

"For everything that was written in the past was written to teach us, so that through the endurance taught in the Scriptures and the encouragement they provide we might have hope."

Romans 15:4

Letter From *Renee

Jurney,

I just read your book. It was the most difficult thing I have ever done next to turning my back on the one person I believed in, my ex-husband, the monster that hurt you so long ago. I'm sure it still feels like it was yesterday, and I'm sorry. I have thought about you and your family almost daily over the last nineteen and a half years. I have prayed, cried, worried, and asked about you. We have most likely talked to many of the same people in the "system" over the years. I have often thought about trying to find you but didn't want to add to your pain. How would I even begin that conversation?

If meeting me is still something you are interested in, just say so. I have always wanted to know that somehow you found God's peace in your life. I am so sorry for the hell he put you through. I wish I could have recognized it in him, prevented it, found him the help he so desperately needed before he hurt you. I wish I had known the demons he had hidden. If I don't hear from you I will certainly understand. All in God's time.

Renee

"I wait for the Lord, my whole being waits, and in His word I put my hope."

Psalm 130:5

An Unsettling Silence

I once wrote that I sometimes think about finding *Mr. Smith's ex-wife so I can give her a great, big hug and tell her how grateful I am for what she did all those years ago. Without her help the police might have never caught him. Who knows how many more lives he would have shattered if she hadn't been brave enough to step forward? I cannot imagine how difficult that must have been for her.

Over the years, I've wondered about her. I've wondered how she was doing. Was she as broken as I was? Did she hide behind a smile too? How did she learn to trust again? I have always thought of her as another one of *Mr. Smith's victims...and I still do. I've always thought I would have so much to say to her if I ever found her, but six days ago, I received a letter from *Mr. Smith's ex-wife, Renee and I have yet to respond to her.

The fact that she had the courage to send it to me makes it that much more amazing. She's probably worried that she upset me since I haven't written back yet and I feel bad about that but I just can't find the right words.

Her words were kind, sincere, beautiful and I loved them. Knowing that she has thought of me as often as I have thought about her was comforting. What's even more comforting to me is knowing that she loves God and has learned to rely on Him the way I have. We were hurt by the same man but we were healed by the same God.

So why haven't I responded to her? I don't know! Usually when I'm ready to write, my words come easily but I am drawing a blank. I find my silence most unsettling.

"May the God who gives endurance and encouragement give you the same attitude of mind toward each other that Christ Jesus had, so that with one mind and one voice you may glorify the God and Father of our Lord Jesus Christ."

Romans 15:5-6

An Unexpected Peace

Renee,

I am so sorry it took me this long to write you back. I hope you haven't been worried that your letter upset me. If you were, let me assure you that it did not. I am so grateful that you reached out to me. I didn't immediately respond because your letter touched me in ways I wasn't prepared for.

I know I wrote in my book that I often think about finding you so I can tell you just how grateful I am, and that's true. Over the years, I have thought about you and your family often. I wondered how you were doing and how this has changed you. I wondered what kind of woman you are today vs. the woman you were then. I always thought I would have so much to say to you and ask you.

After I read your letter I started to respond right away, but several times, I would write a few sentences, and then

Diana Oakley

delete them because they didn't seem to portray what I really felt. Then I'd write something entirely different, and then I'd delete that one. I just couldn't figure out exactly what I wanted to say to you. But it has been over a week and I don't want to keep you hanging on worrying about how your letter has affected me.

I think your letter is amazing! I re-read it every day and every day I still get emotional...but it's a good kind of emotional. I love that we have both found peace and shelter through God. My faith in God is the only thing that has helped me all these years.

You said that you wish you could have recognized his demons and prevented him from hurting me. I hope that doesn't mean that you harbor any guilt for what he did to me. Even if you did recognize anything in him, he is the only person responsible for his actions. I have NEVER blamed you for a second and I hope you've never blamed yourself. Thank you again for having the courage to send me your letter. It has brought a little more peace into my life.

"He has made everything beautiful in its time."

Ecclesiastes 3:11

All in God's Time

For the past nineteen and a half years, I have been dealing...or rather I have been suppressing and NOT dealing...with what happened to me. For the majority of those years, I have not done well. However, the past few years have been a lot better. Ever since I opened up and started writing and talking about how I was raped, I feel like a completely different person. I would have never thought that I would be where I am today. I could never have imagined myself standing in front of groups of women and telling them my story. I wouldn't even talk about it to anyone.

I think another amazing thing that has come out of sharing my story is all the wonderful people I have met or reconnected with. I have helped and counseled others who are in pain and I have made new friends. Remember the letter I received from my kidnapper's ex-wife? How amazing was that?!? We have written back and forth a few times already and we both feel blessed for having found each other. Through our correspondence, I have had the good fortune to connect with someone else; *Mr. Smith's daughter; the one who was only two years old when I was kidnapped. She gave me permission to share her initial letter with you.

Jurney,

Hello. (I've always wanted to say that to you). My mom told me you wrote a book. I go to college two hours away from home, but this weekend I'm going home to read it. I almost had it overnighted to me here at school, but mom told me to just wait and save my money (I'm a poor college kid. :/

I don't really know what to say, I don't want to say too much too soon. I do want you to know that I think about you as much as I think about my family. I grew up knowing everything that happened and I have a few memories of my own. I almost feel as though you are a part of my family, just a relative I've never met; one of those circumstances where family is torn apart by something horrific.

Knowing that there isn't hatred towards my mom and me on your behalf has lifted a HUGE weight off of my shoulders. I feel more at ease, and I don't feel like my mom and I are alone anymore. I've seen my mom cry a lot, and I have cried a lot as well. You're always in our thoughts and prayers. I thank God everyday for making us all strong women. Thank you for reaching out to me, it means more than you know :)

With Love,
Tara

"You intended to harm me, but God intended it for good to accomplish what is now being done, the saving of many lives."

Genesis 50: 20

April 28, 2011

April 28th...Is there anybody else out there that thinks of April 28th as significant? Is there anybody else out there that counts the days in April until the 28th is upon them?

I used to think of April 28th as a day of mourning. I would mope around all day feeling sorry for myself. I would think about all of the directions my life might have taken if only I had stayed home on April 28, 1991 instead of taken that infamous bike ride. If only I hadn't gone off on my own that day, then maybe I wouldn't have been kidnapped. If only I had listened to my gut when it tried to warn me. All of the "if onlys" used to focus around me and how what happened to me could have been avoided "if only".

But now that I have told my story, I feel like maybe all of this had a purpose. Maybe I went through this because God knew I was strong enough to handle it. Maybe if it hadn't happen to me then it would've happened to someone else and maybe that girl wouldn't have dealt with it as well, or maybe she wouldn't have made it out at all. What I'm trying to say is...I'd rather it happened to me than to someone else, especially someone younger than I was. I wouldn't will what happened to me on someone else just to save myself the pain. That would be wrong! It happened to me and, like I said before, I'm not grateful but I am stronger.

I have been praying for healing...well, probably since April 28, 1991. Healing, that never seemed to come. I began to think that maybe I wasn't meant to be healed. Maybe I was meant to keep the pain close to my heart. If it was still painful it would be easier to help others who are in that kind of pain. I could relate to them better. So, I thought I was supposed to share my story solely for the purpose of helping people, but here I am at the end of my journey and I've realized that it's so much more than that. I've realized that writing this book was not only to help others. It was an answer to my prayer. Writing this book was to heal me! I finally feel healed.

I know it will still affect me. After all, we are all molded by the things around us. We are molded by our situations and our experiences. They shape who we are and who we are to become. But as long as we learn from our pasts instead of live in them we will continue to grow. We cannot allow what has happened to us to define who we are. I am so much more than the girl who was raped. You are so much more than the mother who has lost her child. And you are so much more than the wife and the daughter of a monster.

Isn't it amazing how God can take the things in our lives that have hurt us the most and use them for our, as well as His benefit? You may have to wait a very long time before you realize what that benefit is but it will happen. You just need to be patient. Sometimes God answers your prayers, sometimes He doesn't, and sometimes He says, "Not yet". Waiting on the Lord is one of the most difficult things to do. I don't know why God does the things He does but I do know that only He knows what is best for us.

It has been twenty years since I was abducted and raped. I have lived most of those years in fear of a man who is behind bars. I have been letting him control me still. Because of him, I thought I would never be a "normal" person. I thought I was damaged beyond repair. I didn't think I could be helped. But I have come a long way since April 28, 1991. And while today is still a day of reflection and sadness for me, it has evolved into a day of joy as well; a day of joy because I am no longer that broken little girl who cowers in corners; a day of joy because I have learned how to deal with my pain instead of suppress it; a day of joy because if this never happened to me I might not have turned to God for help; a day of joy because I have finally learned how to forgive.

Twenty years is a long time for someone to hide their pain. If you happen to be one of the millions of people in this country who are hiding their pain behind a smile, I want you to know that you are not alone! I spent half of my life hiding behind a smile and I do not recommend it.

So, let's transform April 28. Instead of it being the anniversary of the day I was kidnapped, raped and almost murdered, let's make it a day of transformation, hope and forgiveness. We could think of some clever little name for it and years from now we would hear people say "Happy _____!" I don't know.

What I do know is that I will no longer mope around on April 28. I will instead choose to remember my "jurney" and all of the things I've learned along the way. I hope you too take this day to reflect on your life and remember to count your blessings.

Have you ever noticed that as a whole we give up on God too fast? Aren't you glad He doesn't give up on us as easily?

Thank you, Lord, for never giving up on me.

Letter to Mr. Smith

Mr. Smith,

I am angry with you for what you did to me. I will never forget what you did or how you made me feel, but I want you to know that I forgive you. It took me a long time to realize that if I forgive you it won't make me forget what you did. I thought the two went hand in hand. I thought that with forgiveness comes forgetting and without forgetting how could I truly forgive? But I know now that I don't need to forget in order to forgive.

It took me a long time to realize that I didn't want to forget. I learned many valuable lessons because of what you did to me. I'm not saying that I'm thankful. Please don't misunderstand me. I have simply chosen to learn from my past instead of live in it.

Only God knows the person I could have become had our paths never crossed. Would I have been a better person? I certainly would have been a different person, but better? I don't know. I no longer dwell on it. I love the person I have become and I give God all the credit for that.

I pray that someday you will learn to know and to love God as I have come to know and love Him. Until that day, I will continue to pray for you. I forgive you!

Sincerely,
Jurney Eve

Set Me Free

I use the hand upon my arm,
To write of your intended harm...
The hand you tied to torture me,
But see, your torture set me free....

I use the mouth upon my face,
To share your act of such disgrace...
The mouth you gagged to torture me,
But see, your torture set me free....

I use the ears upon my head,
To listen to others, feeling lost and dead...
The head you struck to torture me,
But see, your torture set me free....

I use my God, Who died for me;
He carries me when it's hard to see....
The God I questioned when you tortured me,
But see, your torture set me free....

You intended me harm, and you could have won,
But, my life is MY journey, and I'm not yet done.

I'm sharing my story, I'm spreading THE WORD,
I'm winning the battle, in case you've not heard...
I've gone from VICTim to VICTory,
Because see, your torture set me free!!

– Stacie Lewis

4/28/2011

About the Author

Diana Oakley is a professional speaker, a member of RAINN's Speakers Bureau (Rape, Abuse and Incest National Network) and the Chairman of the Victim Service Center of Central Florida's Speakers Bureau. Her book, Intended Harm, has been utilized by universities, victim service agencies, law enforcement agencies, various ministries and other organization who work to bring public awareness of sexual assault and the effects it has on its victims.

Diana currently lives in central Florida with her husband and their three children.